Real Life Skills

Giving you the skills for a more productive, happier life full of success and enjoyment

Copyright © 2016-23 Maaaddy Enterprises Inc.

Excerpts from this publication may be reproduced under license from Maaaddy Enterprises Inc. or with the express written permission of Maaaddy Enterprises Inc., or as permitted by law.

All rights reserved, and no part of this publication may be reproduced, stored in a retrieval system, or transmitted in any form or by any means, electronic, mechanical, photocopying, scanning, recording, or otherwise except as specifically authorized.

Maaaddy Enterprises Inc.
Delaware, Ontario, Canada
http://www.reallifeskills.com

Writers: Derek Graystone, Yvette Graystone
Cover Design: Derek Graystone
Layout and Design: Derek Graystone

ISBN: 978-0-9950776-9-0

Ready for Success?

This workbook is about success — your success at school but even more than that. This book is about your ultimate success in life!

You deserve to have a successful life. Success in school, health, happiness, family, work, and finances — even if all that seems a long way away.

School should be about preparing you for success in all of these things and that is what this workbook does. It gets you ready for life.

No matter what path you choose in life, the skills you will learn in this workbook will help you have a more successful life.

Start today by turning to the back of the book and putting in your first success in your SUCCESS LOG! Read all about it on page 142.

> Here is your first entry for your Success Log:
>
> TODAY I STARTED ON MY JOURNEY TO SUCCESS!

Many of these skills build from year to year and so some might seem like review. But these skills need practice, they need focus, and they need you to use them in order to activate the success they represent.

This book is about a better you and a better life. So, let's get to work and start your successful life!

We Make Our Happiness

You Don't Get Happiness – You Create Happiness

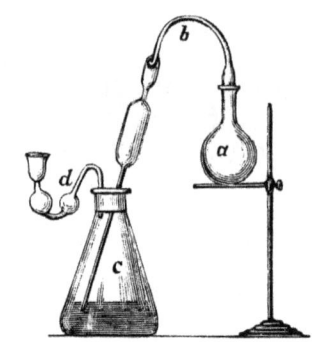

We all want to be happy but what do most of us do about it?

We sit around expecting someone to make us happy.

Because we are taught happiness is something that "happens" to you. It is something that you "find". It is something that just is there or it isn't and there is nothing we can do about it. That is all wrong and there is science to back it up.

> There are 3 rules for happiness:
> 1) You create Happiness – it doesn't just find you
> 2) Happiness is a science and you can make it happen
> 3) Happy people learn faster, live longer, and are more successful

> So how can we get happiness?
> - We have to work for it – yes, happiness takes work.
> - We have to be ready to accept it – happiness can take funny forms.
> - We have to believe we deserve it – everybody deserves to be happy.

Science of Happiness

Most people think they will be happy when things are all the same and we don't get any surprises but that isn't true.

Science shows we need 4 things to be happy

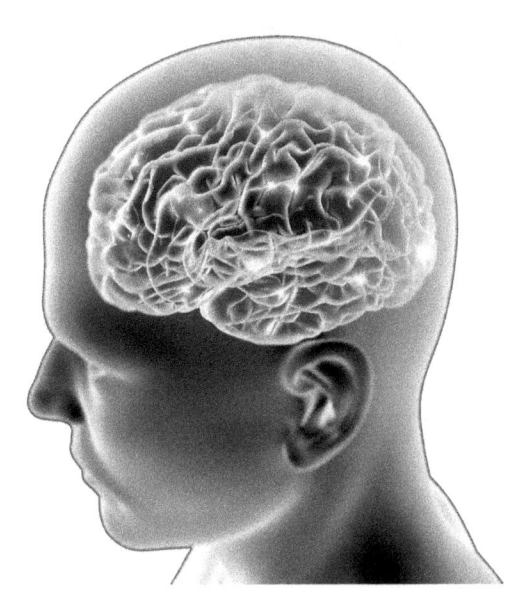

New

Brain scans show we like things that are new. Think about your favorite movie. You might watch it over and over but nothing beats the first time you watched it. Your brain likes surprises (as long as they are welcome surprises).

Challenge

We also like to be challenged. I know, you don't like begin challenged at school but I bet you like it when a video game challenges you. You want to beat the game but you don't like it when the game is too easy.

Creativity

We also like to be creative. We are happiest when we are creating something, or creatively solving a problem.

Sharing

Finally, we are happiest when we have connections to other people. We love to share with others, spend time with other people.

So, do you want to be really happy? So you need to find new, challenging, and creative things you can do with your friends.

Make Your Happiness

If it takes things that are NEW, CHALLENGING, CREATIVE, and SHARED to be happy but what do you have planned?

New — What NEW things are you going to try?
1)
2)
3)

Challenging — What CHALLENGES are you going to face?
1)
2)
3)

Creative — How are you going to use your CREATIVITY?
1)
2)
3)

Shared — Who are you going to share these new experiences with?
1)
2)
3)

Our Daily Happiness

If we create our own happiness, what is the key?

HOW do we create happiness?

Luckily, since so many people want to be happy, scientists have spent some time and money on just that topic. Thanks to advances in neuroscience (which includes the study of how the brain works) and brain scans, we can now look at brains and see what happens when they are happy.

Once we know what happens when they are happy, researchers can try to duplicate the "happiness" reactions and make them stronger.

More research is being done every day but scientists already know some of the important things about being happy. They have used use some of what they know to suggest some simple daily exercises to increase your levels of happiness.

Exercise

Get some physical exercise. That doesn't mean you have to hit the gym but it does mean you have to get up and move around. Play a game, go for a walk, do something to get your blood flowing. 20-30 minutes of physical activity every day will help elevate your mood. Feeling down? Go for a walk and you will feel better.

Be Grateful

Science proves you can't be sad and be grateful at the same time. So every day (yes, that is what daily means,), think of new things that you are grateful for. That can be someone in your family, a special meal you had, a video game, a good mark at school, whatever. Write down things you are grateful for and actually FEEL the gratitude. Be thankful and let the joy of having whatever it is, in your life.

Meditate

You are learning about meditation in this course and how you can write your own guided meditations. Take time in your day to meditate and focus on your goals. Feel the joy it brings you when you have achieved your goals. Visualize how amazing you will feel when that goal is yours.

Be Kind

Do a simple act of kindness every day. Hold a door for someone, pick up something they have dropped, compliment someone on how good they look. Just do something nice for someone every day, the earlier in the day, the better.

Journal

You should be journaling often anyway but also write down something good that happened to you every day. Relive that something on paper. It only has to be a couple lines but reliving it will bring the joy back into your life.

Claim your right to be happy and CREATE your happiness every day!

You can change your mood — your emotion!

List 10 things that change your mood

and make you feel better.

1)

2)

3)

4)

5)

6)

7)

8)

9)

10)

Gratitude Page

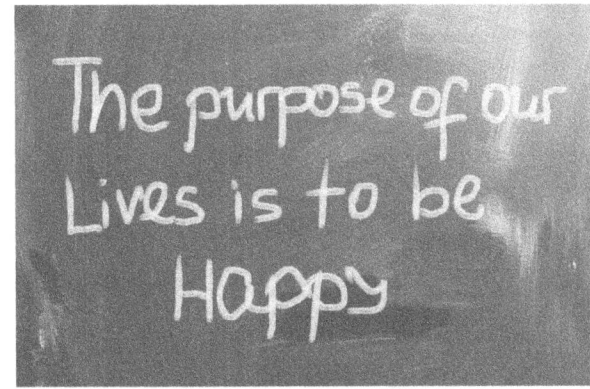

As you go through this workbook, you will see a special symbol on some of the pages that looks like this:

That means you should go back to the next page and write down one new thing you are grateful for.

You might be grateful for your parents or siblings.

You might be grateful for a good mark.

You might be grateful for the nature that surrounds you.

You might be grateful for the new skill you have learned.

You might be grateful for your teacher.

Feel the gratitude!

Don't just write it down, really experience the gratitude and enjoy the feeling of being grateful for everything you have. You might want to even go and thank the person who brought this special thing into your life.

Build a wall of happiness with gratitude!
Fill a Brick with a gratitude (or two or three)

Build a wall of happiness with gratitude!
Fill a Brick with a gratitude (or two or three)

Flexibility
It Isn't Just For Sports

When we think of flexibility, we think about making sure our muscles are limber so we don't hurt ourselves.

But flexibility also refers to our brain and the way we think. Flexibility in our thinking will allow us to tackle challenges from different directions which helps increase the chances we can find a solution.

But we always do it this way!

We need to be prepared to do things a different way, especially if something isn't working out. We aren't born that way, you can train your brain to be flexible. You can exercise your brain and have it accept different ways to do things — make yourself more flexible. It will also help strenghten your brain by creating new pathways. That is called Neural Plasticity. The more pathways you have in your brain, the stronger your creativity, flexibility and adaptability. Try some of these brain exercises to prepare your brain for flexibility and change.

- Pick something you know how to do and do it differently. Eat your dinner with your non-dominant hand. (You non-dominant hand is the one you don't write with).

- Walk to school a different way (make sure your parents know).

- Make up new rules for games.

- Play a word game where you find two different meanings for the same word.

Time for Action –

List 5 things that you always do the same.

1)

2)

3)

4)

5)

Time for Action –

Rewire your brain!

How can you change how you do those 5 things?

1)

2)

3)

4)

5)

Universal Laws

What is Impossible?

We all know about what is impossible. Universal Laws are the rules that make successful people seem to do the impossible.

There are two kinds of laws. Man-made Laws and Universal Laws.

Man-Made Laws

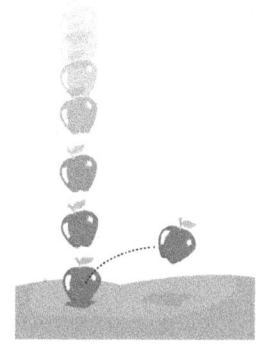

Man-Made Laws are created by man. If you break man-made laws (NOT recommended) you may or may not get caught depending on who sees you. And the laws change from place to place, country to country. What is illegal in New York might not be illegal in Tokyo.

Universal Laws

Universal Laws are not created; they simply exist and always have. That means that no matter where you go, what you do, they are always in effect. If you break the Universal Laws, you always get caught because they are always in force.

Physical Universal Laws

You have already learned about some of the physical universal laws or at least experienced them. Universal physical laws such as gravity, for instance. Gravity works wherever you are — whether you want it to or not. You met gravity when you first learned to walk and when you first learned to ride a bike. At that time, you had no idea what gravity was but you still fell, didn't you? That is the law of gravity at work — it works even if you had never heard of gravity. And whether you fall in New York or Tokyo, the same thing is going to happen.

We can also use the law of gravity because it is always there and we can depend on it. Many of our games rely on gravity. Golf would be hard to play if you hit the ball and it just went off into space. OK, that might be fun but it would be a totally different game.

The point is, whether you want the ball to come down or not, it will because gravity is a law.

Mental Universal Laws

The mental Universal Laws work the same way. The will effect you whether you believe in them, whether you know their names, or even if you know how they work. For good or bad, just like gravity, the laws are always working. If you learn the laws, your life will be easier and more successful.

However, to really benefit from the Universal Laws, you have to understand how they work and how you can make them work for you.

We will eventually learn 10 Universal Laws later in the workbooks.

> Universal Laws are all about the right mindset

Law of Habit

What is the Law?

Everything we do, all the actions and behaviours (good and bad), are based on habits we have developed over the years. We have learned to do everything we do.

How Does it work?

Good and bad activities and behaviours all come out of our habits that we develop over the years.

So many of the things that we do, we do because it has become a habit. Some habits are good (saying "Thank you" whenever someone gives you something) and some habits are bad (playing your video game instead of doing your homework).

We are not born with any habits. Every habit (good and bad) we have is learned by our reactions and responses.

How Can I make it work for me?

All habits are learned. That is good news for us because that means that we can change our habits. We can replace habits we don't like with ones that are better for us!

The first step is to decide what habit you want to change. Think about what habits are hurting your success. Are you putting off doing your homework and you are rushing and making mistakes? Do you need to spend more time studying?

What would you like to change? Work on just habit at a time.

Once you decide what habit you want to change, use the IF-THEN planning method to change your habits.

GOAL

IF

THEN

IF-THEN STATEMENT:

It takes about 30 days for something to become a habit so don't give up, keep at it and you will be successful!

Habit Tracker

A Habit Hack

Jerry Sienfeld is one of the most successful comedians EVER!

Three of his secrets of success is his passion, practice, and dedication. He loves what he does. As he has said, if you are good at something and love doing it, it isn't work. He spent (and still spends) years on the road practicing his Stand Up comedy.

Finally, he is dedicated. For years, Seinfeld has written a joke every day. And, he says, it isn't enough to just write a joke a day. You have to track it.

Don't Break the Chain

For Jerry Sienfeld, not breaking the chain means putting an X on the calendar every day you write a joke. After a week, you have this big line of X's. After a month, it is a big block. Everytime you see that big bunch of X's you are motivated not to Break The Chain.

At the back of the book are several Habit Trackers. Each day that you do whatever your new habit is, put an X on that day. For instance, let's say you are trying to make your bed every day. Every time you make your bed in the morning, make an X on the calendar. Try to see if you can keep the chain going for as long as possible. If you do break the chain, don't worry. Just start again and see you can go longer next time!

How To Set Goals and Plan For Success

What Is A Goal?

A goal is not just a task or something you have to do. How do you know the difference? To be a true goal, there must be some obstacle in your way to accomplish your goal.

TASK	GOAL (and obstacle)
Eating lunch	Eating a nutritious lunch every day is a goal (takes planning & self-discipline)
Going to bed every night	Going to bed every night by 10 (giving up some videos or games)
Doing your homework	Doing your homework BEFORE you watch videos (you need self-discipline)

Goals always take self-discipline to attempt and succeed. To achieve a goal, you must take ACTION and that will mean decision-making and self-discipline. Luckily, you learn strategies for both here.

Goals can involve:

- achieving something you haven't done before
- becoming a better person
- learning or mastering a new skill or ability
- breaking an old bad habit or developing a new good habit
- earning something that you really want — yes, goals can be something material that you want but you will notice it was last on the list!

What your goal should be in order to be worthwhile and successful...

Believe

You must BELIEVE that you can achieve the goal.

It doesn't matter if anyone else believes it is possible as long as you do! You can set big goals but they have to be realistic enough or you will just give up long before you ever achieve them.

You must balance between too big a goal and something too easy.

Start by setting smaller goals while you build your goal setting and success planning muscles.

Build your confidence and then you can begin tackling even bigger goals!

Measurable

Someone else has to be able to measure it. Whether it is a certain number of points scored in a game, a particular grade in math, or a certain number of push-ups. You must be able to measure the success of your goal!

Be Specific

Don't say, "I want an A or a B on this test", or "I want to score more in this game". There cannot be an alternative unless it is something even better. It is this goal and no other. "I will get an A on my next Math test or even better."

All For You

The goal must be what you want and not what someone else wants. Other people may benefit from you achieving your goal (I want to raise $500 for the Cancer Research Fund) but it has to be because you want to achieve the goal. Why is very important when you are considering your goal. If your WHY is not big enough, it will be very hard to achieve your goal.

Do You Have Control?

You must have control over the goal. Remember your Circle of Control. The only thing you can change is yourself. You can't change the weather, you can't change the colour of the sky, and you sure can't change somebody else.

You can't try to achieve something that is out of your control. You can't want a goal that depends on changing how someone else behaves. "I want this person to like me more." That is the recipe for frustration!

Don't Hurt Anyone Else

Your goal is all about you but don't ignore others. You are a good person, with a good caring character. Your goal must not hurt anyone else. What does that mean?

> Goal: Win more basketball games
> (that would be a fine goal)

> **Good**
>
> Practice more and get better and you beat the other team

> **Bad**
>
> Hurt the other team's star player and win the game.

Why Should You Set A Goal?

"You can't hit a target you can't see."

Goals are like a road map in life. Goals give you a direction in life like an internal GPS.

If you aren't moving toward the goal, your internal GPS should be screaming "DANGER – YOU ARE OFF-COURSE."

By having goals to follow, you develop meaning and direction in your life. You enjoy life to the fullest because you are always moving forward, pushing toward your fulfillment and, ultimately, your happiness. There we go, trying to make you happy again.

Set your Destination!

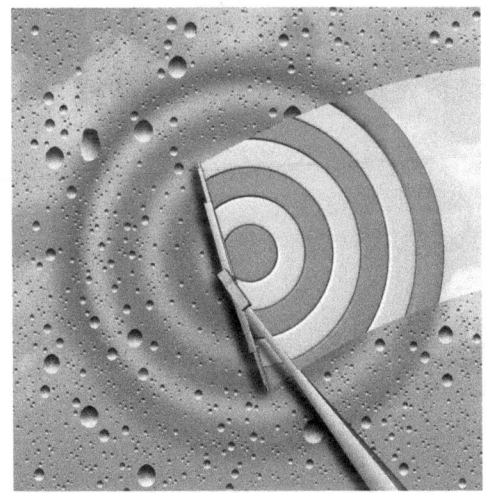

If you don't know where you are going, any road will get you there. If you don't have a specific goal or goals in life, you will just drift.

Clean off your vision because drifting leads to boredom and unhappiness. Setting and achieving goals brings happiness – and we all want to be happy, right? I think I might have mentioned that. But if you want a roadmap for your life, you must to have a destination.

If you are going to achieve anything, you have to decide what is important to you. What is worth your effort? What will make you feel happy?

And how will you get what is important to you?

It will take work to achieve what you want.

And the more you want, the harder you will have to work.

You will have to give something up (time, energy, an activity you like) to achieve your goal.

So make sure your goal is what you really want and it is going to be worth the work.

The Science of Goal Setting

The good news — people have been studying how to reach goals for a long, long time. There is a science behind setting goals and creating a plan to be successful.

All these totally awesome scientists have spent hours tracking people and their goals, peeking into their brains, and coming up with a list of things that actually work for the majority of the successful people in the world.

So, how can you become one of the successful people?

Follow the steps (check out the Law of Cause and Effect on page 54 because "success leaves tracks").

7 Easy Goal Setting Steps

Step #1 - Decide on a goal with a deadline

Set a goal that:

- is something YOU want
- is something you BELIEVE you can do — eventually
- gets you excited
- will give your life meaning
- will be the first thing you think about in the morning

When do you usually study for a test or start an assignment? Just before it is done? Most people do.

We like deadlines because they motivate us so set a deadline for your goal. Give yourself enough time to be able to achieve your goal but not too much time so you slack off.

Write down the goal and be very clear on what the goal is. Write it as though you have already achieved your goal.

Wrong: ~~I will pass my math test~~
Right: I have received an A on my math test on multiplication.

Wrong: ~~I will do better in basketball.~~
Right: I just broke my record for most points scored in a game by 10 points.

Step #2 - Identify reasons for the goals

This is a key step. Why do you want this goal? You must be able to come up with strong, burning reasons for wanting to achieve your goal.

Big Reasons = Motivation

If you can't come up with many big reasons for achieving this goal, you will give up when things get hard. And, if it is a big enough goal, things will get hard.

Write down all the reasons you want to achieve the goal.

- be specific
- feel the emotions achievement will bring
- list the people this goal might help

Who else will your goal help? If you get better grades, your parents will be proud of you. If you get better grades, your teacher will feel proud of you and themselves. If you get better grades, you will inspire others to get better grades.

If you just can't come up with big reasons, go back to step 1 and get a new goal – this might not be the goal for you right now.

When the going gets tough (and it always does), you can motivate yourself by reading over this list of reasons why you want your goal.

Step #3 - Identify obstacles

All worthwhile goals will have obstacles or challenges.

Obstacles are things that stand in your way and prevent you from achieving your goal – like big and small boulders in the road. And just like the boulders in the road, you can either go around them, move them, or just blast right through them.

Obstacles can be internal or external.

Internal obstacles are often your own limiting beliefs that say "I can't do this". It could be your refusal to work hard or study longer.

External obstacles might be a lack of money, a lack of enough people to help you, or even something like not having a basketball to practice with.

Think about all the things that are standing in your way. DON'T try to solve these challenges yet. Just make a detailed list all the obstacles.

Be honest and make sure you include the obstacles like "I don't think I can do this...so I won't be successful." YOU just might be the biggest obstacle you have to overcome. Believe in yourself. Decide that you can accomplish anything you put your mind to. The impossible just takes longer.

Step #4 - Identify required knowledge

What don't you know? A lack of knowledge can be a big obstacle.

What things are you going to have to learn to achieve your goal?

Sometimes, the knowledge you need will come from someone else, so don't think you have to know everything to achieve your goal. You might have to turn to experts and that is OK because that is the next step.

Don't try to solve the challenges or start trying to accumulate the knowledge. Just list all the things you will need to know in order to be successful.

Step #5 - Identify people required

You don't have to do everything alone! Everyone who has ever achieved a goal has had help along the way.

Don't be afraid to ask for help.

The smartest people in the world are the people that ask for help when they need it!

Whose help are you going to need to achieve your goal?

It might be your parents, your teacher, or your friends. Maybe it is a friend of a friend. Or maybe, it is someone you don't even know, yet.

Maybe you need to find someone who has expert knowledge.

List everyone and don't be afraid to ask for help. Good leaders surround themselves with people who are smarter than they are.

When asking for help, first think about what you can do for the person who is going to help you. For everyone you are going to ask for help, find something you can do for them first.

> It is NOT
> "ASK and you will receive".
> It is
> "GIVE and you will receive".

Unconditionally give something first (that means you give it freely even if they don't help you) and then seek help from that person. What if they don't help you? So what? At least you feel good giving something. Just find somebody else that can help you and figure out what you can give that person.

> Now the fun begins!

Step #6 - Devise a plan

It is solution time! Time to creatively turn all those obstacles and challenges into opportunities to learn, discover, and conquer.

Create a plan using Steps #2-5.

How can you go around, go over, or blast through those obstacles?

Where are you going to find the knowledge you need? What are you going to give those people you will need help from?

Your plan becomes a long list of solutions and opportunities.

Once you have those solutions, arrange the list in the order you will do them. There will always be things you need to do first, second, and third. Now, you have the plan that you just have to follow. All that is left to do is GET STARTED!

> Start on something today and then do at least one thing every day to move you closer to your goal.

If you don't know where to start ... start on the hardest thing first.

What???

Yes! Start on the thing that you totally DO NOT want to do. Get that over with and you will never have to think about it again.

Step #7 - Visualize and emotionalize

You are already doing something from your list every day.

The other thing to do every day is think about your goal.

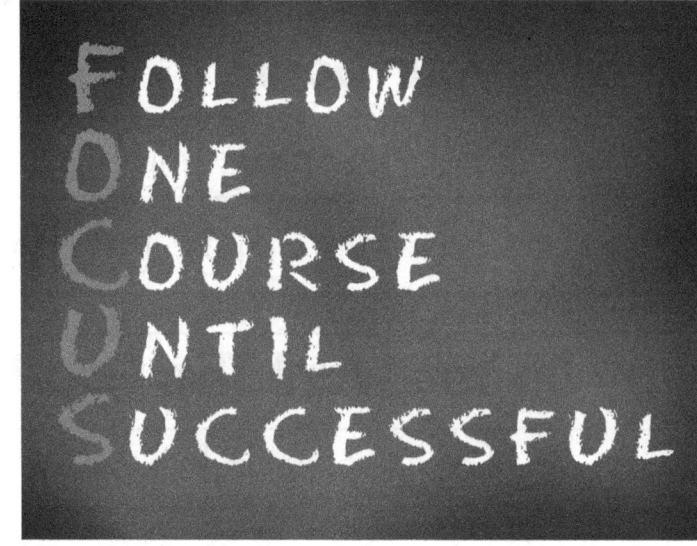

Visualize yourself already successful. Use your meditation time to think about your goal as complete. Feel what the end will be like. Imagine the joy and excitement. Imagine sharing your success with others. Feel the pride — YES, it is OK to be proud of yourself and your successes.

Every day, as you read your goal, imagine all those reasons you wrote in Step #2.

Convince yourself you have completed your goal.

Your subconscious will take over and help move your goal toward you as you move toward your goal.

You could also use your new skill of writing affirmations to write something about your goal that you could repeat to yourself several times a day.

NOW IT IS TIME TO PRACTICE THESE SKILLS!

Example Goal Planning

What is your Goal?

I am sinking one out of every four free throws by the end of the season.

Why Do You Want This Goal?

I get fouled a lot because I am small & more free throws will make me valuable to the team.

What Are Your Obstacles?

My lack of belief in myself
Lack of Practice
I don't have a basket at home

What Knowledge Do You Need?

What am I doing wrong?
How can I improve?

Who Can Help You?

My Coach
My Mom & Dad

Now use this information to create your success plan!

What Is Your Plan?

1) Talk to my coach about how I can improve my free throws & take notes
2) Take notes, watch videos of the pros making free throws & duplicate their motions.
3) Review my notes each day before practice
4) Do extra chores at home to earn a basket for home.
5) Get up 15 min early to do 50 free throws.
6) Practice 150 free throws after school every day (even days I have practice.
7) Ask my coach to review my progress once a week & use his suggestions.
8) Spend 10 min imagining the perfect basket.

See yourself already successful.
Feel what it will be like to have succeeded.
Think about how good you will feel
several times per day.

Never Give Up

Monthly Goal

What is your Goal?

Why Do You Want This Goal?

What Are Your Obstacles?

What Knowledge Do You Need?

Who Can Help You?

Now use this information to create your success plan!

What Is Your Plan?

See yourself already successful.
Feel what it will be like to have succeeded.
Think about how good you will feel
several times per day.

Never Give Up

What to do with a Dollar?

You might ask yourself, what does it matter what you do with a dollar?

Let's say you get some money for your birthday.

You say, "If I have money, I am going to spend it. Candy, games, a movie — doesn't matter what; I am going to make sure I spend every cent of that money."

But, did you know that what you do with a dollar now is going decide what the rest of your life will be like? It will decide:
- how big a house you have
- if you can go on vacations
- how long you will have to work
- how stress free your life is

That's right, what you do with a dollar NOW will affect what the rest of your life will be like because of the Law of Habit.

If you are smart about what you do with a dollar now, you will set the habit that will give you an amazing life:
- free of stress
- full of abundance (You will have lots of money)
- focused on success and happiness

From now on, you will use the

70-10-10-10 Rule!

70-10-10-10 Rule

A dollar is made up of 100 cents. When you get a dollar, you will spend it based on the success formula called the 70-10-10-10 rule.

10 cents of every dollar goes to investment

Money that goes into investment never gets spent. Want to be a millionaire? Investments will get you there.

10 cents of every dollar goes to savings

This is money you put aside in a bank account for something bigger you want in the future. Want to feel secure; a savings account will get you there.

10 cents of every dollar goes to giving

You have a dollar so you should be grateful. Find a charity you like and give them some money. Want more happiness and abundance, giving will get you there.

70 cents of every dollar you get to spend

The rest of the dollar, you get to spend on whatever you need or want. Want to be stress-free, budgeting will get you there.

And this goes for every dollar you get. If you get $10, $1 to investment, $1 to savings, $1 to giving, and you spend $7.

Test Preparation

Nobody likes taking tests.

Do tests make you:

- nervous
- anxious
- completely scared

For that fear, use your meditation techniques to put the test into perspective and calm your mind and body.

How confident do you feel?

How well you think you can do will have a huge impact on your level of anxiety. Get rid of negative thoughts and believe in yourself.

How prepared are you?

This is the most important part of reducing anxiety. Sorry, no quick fix for this one. The only solution here is preparation and proper studying.

> Spending more time each day preparing as you learn will reduce your study time.

Start with good notes

    a. Take good, accurate, complete notes in class. Practice using bullet point notes.

    b. Make sure you have all the formulas, dates, and names your teacher has given you.

    c. Take down of some of the examples in your notes.

    d. Pay attention in class.

        i. Your teacher will often emphasize or flat out tell you the most important parts to study.

        ii. Highlight those parts of your notes as Very Important.

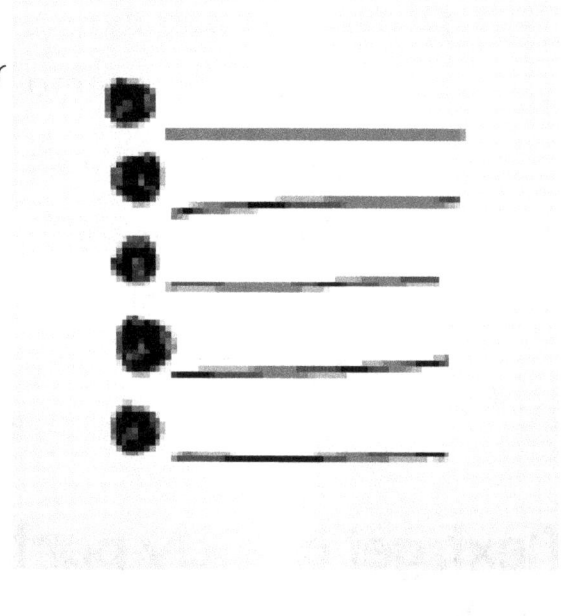

    e. Review your notes each day and make sure you understand what you wrote.

        i. Don't waste study time rewriting study notes. You can read over good notes several times in the time it would take to rewrite your notes.

Start each study session with a couple of minutes of meditation to calm and focus your mind.

    a. Visualize how well you will do on the test and feel confident in how much you know the material.

Study on your own first to become familiar with the topic.

   a. Read over your notes.
   b. Yes, you can play music in the background but don't play videos. Instrumental music (no words) is better.
   c. No, you can't watch videos while you study.
      i. Brains scans show we can only do one thing at a time!
      ii. If you think you can study better with the videos on, you are just fooling yourself because that is easier than using your self-discipline to turn off the videos and just study.

Next, get a study partner (or parent) to go over the material with you.

   a. Use this study time as a question and answer study
   b. Take turns asking questions and try to answer without the study notes.
   c. You can make "Flash Cards" to quiz yourself. Put the question on one side and the answer on the other. Read the question and see if you can answer the question
   d. Make notes of any parts of the material you need to spend more time studying.
   e. Make the sessions short and regular.

Super-Sessions or Mini-Sessions?

Which one works better?

> Long cramming sessions right before the test?

> Short mini-sessions over many days before the test?

We want to believe that long cramming sessions work best because that works with our lack of self-discipline. You always put off studying until you have no choice and MUST study the night before. We take the easy route and then tell ourselves it is the best.

But science says you are wrong.

Everything we know about how the brain works tells us that mini-sessions spread over the days before a test work better. You learn it better and remember it longer.

Understanding versus Memorizing

Use your class time and nightly review of your notes to understand the material rather than just memorize it.

If you can apply the material, rather than just spit it out, it will be easier to remember by test time.

Taking Notes

What is Plagiarism?

With the Internet, it is easy to look up something on a web site and then just cut and paste it into your project.
Way faster than writing it yourself, right?

Do you know what plagiarism is?

That is a fancy way of saying you are stealing someone else's words or ideas. And this can get you a zero on assignments or get you kicked out of University. And that is what you are doing with cutting and pasting. Instead, you need to put it in your own words.

Bullet Points to the rescue

The first step is to summarize what the person has said by putting it into bullet points. These are just short ideas, not even complete sentences. They just give the thoughts or facts. After you collect all your bullet points, you then write it again in your own words. The sentences and paragraphs are yours. If they are new ideas, you do have to tell where you got those ideas. That is called "citing" and you will learn about that in your courses.

For now, we are going to have some practice making bullet points. You will read a short story about some amazing people. Then you will summarize the story — make your own bullet points.

We have helped you out with the first one on page 56. After that, you are on your own (but the answers are at the back).

How to take good summary notes

Read the article, short story, web page, etc. over once or twice to be sure you understand all the ideas the author is presenting.

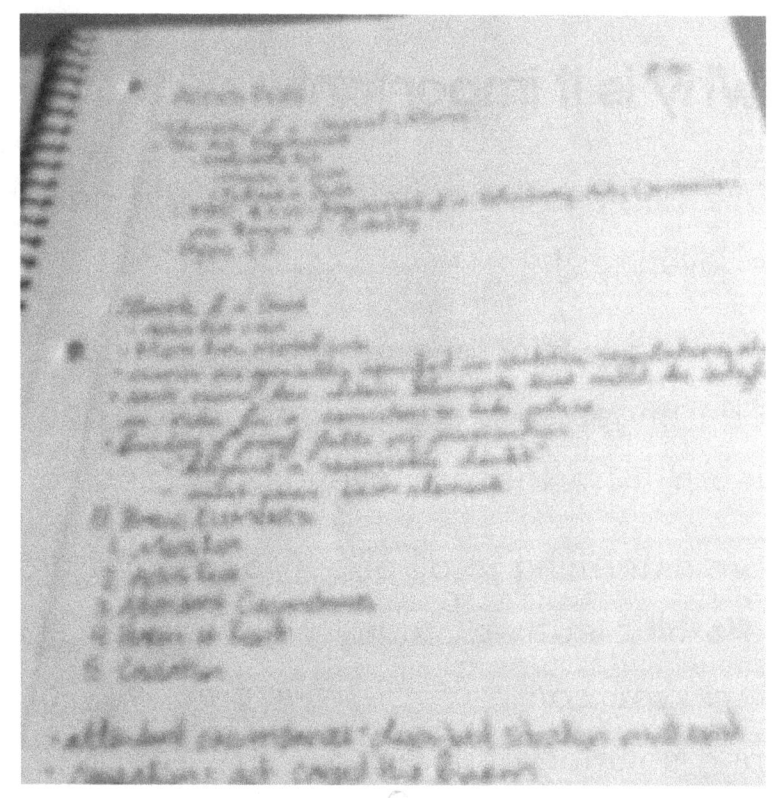

Stick to the key, most important facts. You know the key facts because, if they were missing, nothing would make sense. Why you are summarizing will be key to deciding what you should make notes of. Names and dates might be important. Think of the 5 Ws & How. Who, What, Where, When, Why, & How are all important to take notes about.

You don't have to write down every word. Take a sentence or even a paragraph and summarize with just the key facts.

Taking notes is one time that you don't have to worry about good grammar or complete sentences. Just a few words or sometimes only a single word will convey the idea you need.

When you are finished, review your notes and see if you have all the facts you need.

Brainstorming

Why is it important

We all have problems (you should call them challenges).

A good leader and entrepreneur uses challenges to create opportunities and learn from those challenges by finding solutions.

Brainstorming is all about ideas and creativity. Wait, don't say it...we are all creative — don't sell yourself short. Brainstorming is one way that you can exercise your creativity and widen your mind for idea and solution generation.

Brainstorming is also extremely useful for developing creative ideas for stories, essays, speeches, and projects.

The key behind brainstorming is to capture ideas quickly before your mind has an opportunity to judge if the idea is good or bad — just write the idea down!

Always focus on solutions and you can turn challenges into money. That is what all successful entrepreneurs do.

When to use brainstorming

- Use brainstorming any time you need to come up with a variety of solutions or ideas.
- Brainstorm ideas on creating a topic for an essay or a project.
- Brainstorm ideas for the content of your essay.
- Use brainstorming to come up with ideas for games for your next party or event.

How to Brainstorm

Brainstorming can be done in a variety of ways but there are a few clear steps to take before you actually start brainstorming.

Clearly define your goal

a. What is it you are trying to accomplish? You need to be clear so you can focus on just that idea.
b. Write it down to remind you of your goal
c. Focus your thoughts on your goal

Eat and drink

a. You need brain food if you want to create a good storm up there
b. Drink because dehydration (lack of water) limits how well your brain works

Take your time

    a. Some brainstorming methods force you to work quickly but most require time

    b. This is where you use self-discipline and don't put things off so you don't have time to really work on the idea

    c. Don't have something you have to do right after because too much of your mind will be focused on that and not your brainstorming

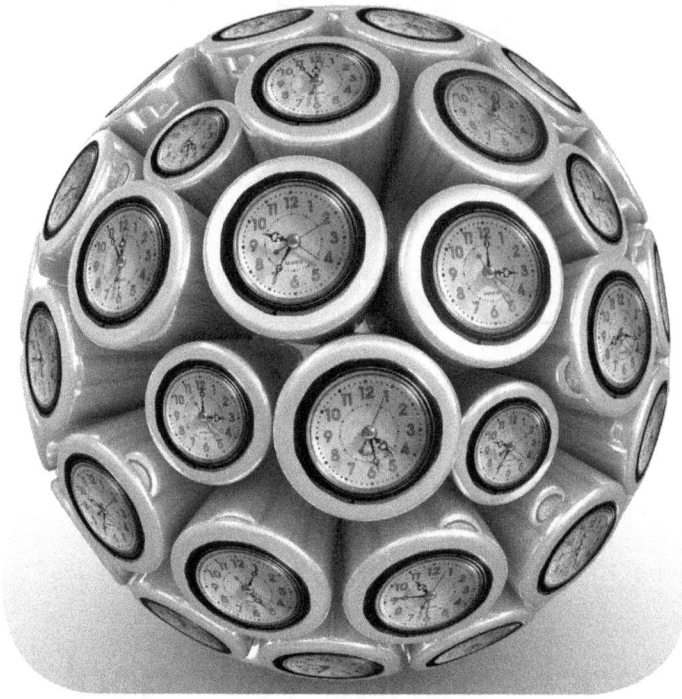

Meditation

    a. Use your meditation skills to calm your mind and stop other thoughts from poking themselves into your brainstorming time

    b. Use meditation to focus on your idea – taking 5 minutes to focus your mind on your challenge or idea is time well spent

Know when to stop

    a. Creativity can't be forced

    b. With practice, you will know when the ideas just aren't coming

    c. But don't let self-doubt convince you that the ideas aren't coming – remember you are a creative being

Know when not to stop

    a. If the ideas are coming, don't stop until they are all dried up – sometimes your best ideas will come after you think you know the solution

Different Brainstorming Methods

There are many many brainstorming methods.

Each year, we remind you of the 3 top methods and then introduce you to a couple new methods. Everybody is unique and some methods will work for you and some won't.

We encourage you to work with a pen or pencil and paper if possible. Computers are great but science has shown us with brain scans that using a pen or pencil fires off the creative parts of the brain.

This course is all about giving you the knowledge and tools to make your life easier. So take advantage of the extra boost that using a pencil gives you.

REMEMBER:

Your number 1 job is to capture as many ideas as you can without judging the idea.

All ideas are valid during brainstorming.

When you think you are out of ideas, try for one more and then quit.

SMARTER GOALS

You may have heard of SMART goals that GE pioneered in the 1980s. We have been taught goals should be Specific, Measured, Attainable, Realistic, and Timed. However, over the last 40 years, research has shown that the system doesn't work.
Michael Hyatt teaches a SMARTER system. This expanded and revised system is backed by the latest scientific research and will help you reach your goals.

S pecific
M easured
A ctionable
R isky
T imed
E xciting
R elevant

S is still for SPECIFIC

Your goals must be specific. Don't say you want better marks – 52 is better than 51. Instead, say, I want to get 80 out of 100 on the next test. Don't say, I want to be better at basketball. Say, I will sink 7 out of 10 baskets. Make sure you can see the goal clearly. Visualize it.

M is still for Measurable

If you can't measure your goal, how will you know you have achieved it? Anyone should be able to walk up and tell if you have reached your goal. Anyone can look at your test and see that you did or did not get an 80.

A is now Actionable

Can you act on your goal? Can you start doing something today? Don't say, "I want to be a writer." Make your goal, "Write a book". Or better, "Write my novel, The Stone Maker". Use action verbs (Write) instead of "to be" verbs (to be a writer).

R is now Risky

Usually A is for attainable and R is for realistic. This goes against the science. Over 400 scientific studies showed that you are 250% more likely to achieve a risky goal than a realistic one. A risky goal is one that makes you a little scared that you can't do it. A risky goal is one that you don't really know how to achieve it. You are more likely to achieve a risky goal because it challenges and motivates you. Not knowing how you are going to achieve your goal is a good thing. Don't worry, you will figure it out.

T is now for Time-Keyed

You need a deadline or you will procrastinate (put things off). You may have done a project the night before it was due (bad idea). Would you have done it that night if the teacher said, "You have another week?" No! So set a deadline and it should be a little uncomfortable and push you. (See R for Risky for the motivation that challenge brings you.) Or if your goal is a habit goal, then the time key would be the WHEN. Run 1 km every Monday, Wednesday, & Saturday at the park.

E is for Exciting

A goal has to excite you. If it doesn't excite you, it is just a project. Spending more time studying wont' excite you but getting your best mark ever will! Exciting goals will motivate you when you are stuck in the work. Yes, goals will require work. With excitement, you will have the motivation to finish.

R is for Relevant

The goal has to be relevant to what is happening in your life. What if you are in the middle of exams? Now might not be the time to be starting a new goal of increasing your basketball skills. You just won't be successful. Either you will do poorly on your exams or you will become discouraged with your new goal because of lack of time. You have to align your goals with your life.

> "The first key difference between an unmet goal and personal success is the belief that it can be achieved."
>
> - Michael Hyatt

Write your Goal from page 36.

[   ]

Is your goal a "SMARTER" goal?

Can you re-write your goal to make it a SMARTER goal? Remember that a SMARTER goal is:

Specific
    Measurable
        Actionalble
            Risky
                Time-keyed
                    Exciting
                      Relavent

Now re-write your Goal and make it a SMARTER goal!

[   ]

Law of Cause and Effect

What is the Law?

The Law of Cause and Effect states that for every effect there is a cause.

How Does it work?

If you want something in your life (some effect), you can track it back the reason it happened (the cause) and make that happen in your life.

Success always leaves tracks.

If you see someone who has been successful in doing something you want, look at their life, their habits, and their activities and you will find out how they achieved their goal.

Once you know the cause, all you have to do is duplicate it and you can have that same success in your life.

The cause is often just a group of steps that you can duplicate if you do it the same way.

How Can I make it work for me?

There are several steps you can take to use the Law of Cause and Effect in your life.

1) Be clear about what you want and write it down to make it a focus.
2) Be mindful and observant of others to see who has success where you want it.
3) Write down the steps you see others taking to achieve success.
4) Duplicate the steps and use persistence to continue because nothing works the first time.
5) Be prepared to share your success. Your tracks can help others achieve.

Example

You have already used the Law of Cause and Effect. When you learned to tie your shoes, you activated the Law. You watched how someone else was successful and duplicated their actions. Eventually, through repetition and practice, you achieved the same success.

Important Additions

The other aspect of the Law of Cause and Effect is that thoughts are causes and success is the effect. Positive thoughts and thinking about what you want, rather than what you don't want, will help to bring about the success you desire.

Cause and Effect

List 5 Cause and Effects. Remember positive and negative thoughts can be causes that have very real effects.

Cause	Effect

Making Decisions

How important are decisions?

Effective leaders make more decisions and make them faster. They might not always be the "right" decision or even the "best" decision. However, as a mark of success, decision making is a clear indicator. Strong leaders make decisions quickly based on the best available information. Should it be the wrong decision, they just as quickly make another decision to fix the problem.

All actions start with a decision.

Nothing happens without action.

You might want to learn how to sink a basket in basketball. You may have a goal to sink ten baskets in a row. You might know where there is a net and a basketball.

But nothing will happen until you pick up that basketball – until you take ACTION.

And no ACTION happens without a DECISION.

A decision is the beginning of all action but decisions without action are the same as not making a decision.

Being Proactive

Making timely decisions also allows you to be "proactive". Proactive means you take action and direct how things happen. You see challenges before they happen and take action to prevent them. You take control of events. If you don't make timely decisions, you will find yourself reacting to events or other people's decisions.

If you are proactive, your life has less stress and moves in the direction of your goals.

You move events toward your desires. (Law of Control)

If you only react to events, you give up your control. You dance to someone else's song, like a puppet on strings. You are always busy putting out fires and never get a chance to move toward what YOU want.

Happiness comes from being proactive, making decisions and taking ACTION.

Cut the strings and control your life by making decisions.

Make sure you listen to your gut.

Real Life Skills will give you several methods to help you make decisions in a logical manner.

These methods help you make good decisions based on the facts. Cold hard facts are important but there is more to making decisions.

You have to listen to your intuition. That is the little voice inside that says, "this feels right" or "this feels wrong". Sometimes that voice goes against logic.

You have to learn to trust your intuition because often this little voice (which really originates in your subconscious) is noticing things that you might have missed in your decision making process.

Or, it could be <u>fear</u> talking.

Recognizing the fear factor

So how do you know if it is intuition or fear?

As you become more aware of your emotions, you will begin to recognize when your intuition is speaking or your fear is speaking. Your fear will be because of your limiting beliefs (Law of Belief) and your self-esteem. As you eliminate your limiting beliefs and increase your self-esteem, your fear voice will diminish and you will be able to trust that quiet voice of true intuition.

> You can only learn to trust your intuition through experience and practicing Emotional Intelligence.

What is Self-Discipline?

Self-discipline is:

> Doing what you should do, when you should do it, whether you want to or not.

That's pretty simple. Doing what you should do, whether you want to or not.

Very simple and very easy to do. So why is it so hard to do?

Because it is also easy NOT to do.

We all have things we love to do and things that we don't love to do. We need self-discipline for the things we DON'T like to do.

We do what we love

Peter loves reading. He always completes his reading homework on time.

Jamie dislikes reading. She rarely gets her reading homework done.

Jamie loves to draw and paint. She always completes her art projects on time.

Peter dislikes art and feels he is a bad painter. He never completes his art projects on time.

Remember this when you find a career:

> Find your passion in life,
> find out
> what you really love to do,
> and then
> find a way to make a living at it.

Why Do I Need Self-Discipline

All through your life, you will have to do things you don't really want to do. Yes, even adults have to do things they don't want to do.

Your life will be easier if you are capable of getting at those things faster.

Your parents have been your self-discipline, reminding you what to do, sometimes forcing you to do things. At school, your teachers are your self-discipline. But soon you will be on your own, you will be working.

"But", you say, "My boss will tell me what to do". WRONG! If your boss has to keep telling you over and over what to do, you won't have to worry about him for long. You will be fired.

Carrying a Heavy Weight All Day

Imagine you have something you don't want to do.

Without self-discipline, you keep putting it off all day and all you can think about is what you have to do.

You carry the heavy weight all day. All day, you can't help but think about doing this awful, terrible, totally rotten thing that you really, really don't want to do.

What kind of day are you going to have?

Now imagine you do that lousy job first and get it over with. It is bad, just like you thought, but not AS bad as you thought.

For the rest of the day, you only have good things to think about.

For the rest of the day, you can take pride in having accomplished that terrible thing.

> You can have a happy day - thanks to self-discipline.

How Can I Practice Self-Discipline

Self-discipline is doing what we should do, when we should do it, whether we want to or not.

That can be really hard sometimes!

You know you should do your homework but it is so much easier to go out and ride your bike, go play basketball, watch TV, or play video games. There are so many distractions.

How do you make yourself do what you are supposed to do?

Just like goal setting, you must have a plan.

If you have a plan, you are way more likely to succeed.

So how do you create a plan to make you more disciplined?

It takes practice to develop the habit (the Law of Habit) and it takes a good plan.

Creating a plan is being proactive — acting BEFORE a problem happens. If you ACT instead of REACT, you take control of your life and make self-discipline even easier. So be proactive and create your plan.

The IF-THEN Plan

Like all good plans, the IF-THEN plan is simple.

> The If-Then plan says:
> If X happens, then I will do Y

How simple is that?

> If it is 4:30, then I will do my homework for an hour.

With that plan, you know that at 4:30, you start doing your homework for an hour. There is no question in the matter, you just do it.

No Excuses, No Changes, No Problem.

This is the single most important thing you can do to make yourself more self-disciplined because all you have to do is follow one simple rule that YOU made up.

Why does this work?

Our brains are hard-wired to think this way. Most things we do force us to think this way.

> If I am hungry, then I eat.
> If I am tired, then I go to sleep.
> If I see a Sabre-Tooth Tiger, then I run away.
> If someone throws something at us, then we duck.

All these things are really habits because that is how we create habits. Habits are just responses to certain things that we have repeated over and over again. They become the only things we ever think to do in that situation. We don't even have to think about it, we just do it. It always just feels natural.

The first time someone threw something at us, we didn't duck and it hit us. We learned and practiced. Now it is a habit and it takes real concentration to just stand there and let yourself get hit.

> # Good Habits and Bad Habits form the same way, so form GOOD habits!

Self-Discipline – Creating Your Own Plan

First, you need a goal — something you want to become a habit — even if it is just for a short time. That might be finishing your homework, always studying a week for before a test, or not stopping my homework just because my favorite show is on.

Now find a trigger (the IF part of the plan). This might be a time (bedtime), a situation (Sabre-Tooth Tiger), or a feeling (hungry).

Now what are you going to do when that IF thing happens? That is the THEN part of the plan (sleep, run, eat).

GOAL
Study for my test every night for a week.

IF
it is 8 pm

THEN
study for 20 min

IF-THEN STATEMENT:
If I have a test within the next week, then I will study at 8 pm every night for 20 minutes.

Do you have the self-discipline to make AND KEEP your plans?

My IF - THEN Plan

GOAL

IF

THEN

IF-THEN STATEMENT:

GOAL

IF

THEN

IF-THEN STATEMENT:

Habit Tracker Reminder

Turn to the end of the book

Remember what Jerry Sienfeld taught as one of the keys to his amazing success!

You have set a couple of goals on the previous page, but how are you going to be sure that you are doing it?

Use the Habit Tracker at the end of the book to track you success.

You might even want to tear a page out of the book and hang it on the wall. That way, you can see your success in front of you every day.

If you tell others about your plan, they can help you stay accountable.

Show your dedication to your habit and be proud of your success.

Don't Break the Chain

Exercise Your Creativity

Why Is Creativity Important?

We think only artists and writers need creativity, but we all use creativity. Doctors, lawyers, detectives, plumbers, coaches, all use creativity to solve problems.

We all have creativity in us, we just have to exercise the muscle more.

Believing that you are creative will take you far in life as you are faced with more and more challenges. Knowing that you can find a solution to any problem will give you the confidence to take on even bigger challenges. The 30 Circles exercise is designed to exercise your creative brain cells.

Set a timer (we will give you 10 minutes) and see how many recognizable objects you can create out of the 30 circles on the next page. Just sketch them out. You can use colour if you like but don't get stuck in the details. You don't have to be an artist.

Here are some examples to get you started. As you can see from my sketches, you really don't have to be an artist. The one on the bottom left is supposed to be a donut with sprinkles.

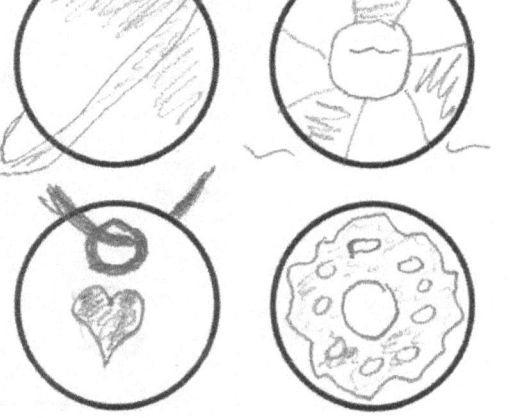

Just have fun!

30 Circles Exercise

Do You Believe in Luck?

Why are some people so lucky?

Why do some people get all the good luck?

Are some people really luckier than other people?

Scientists did an experiment with people who thought they were lucky and those that didn't. They had to pick the toss of a coin. Guess what? Both groups scored the same.

People who think they are lucky just have a better, more positive, outlook on life. They expect good things to happen to them. When bad things happen, they don't get as upset and find good things in the bad – they see the good luck.

People who think they are lucky show how positive they are. People like and trust positive people because they want the "luck" to be transferred to them. So, "lucky people" are given more opportunities. Once again, they bring their own luck.

Finally, being given more opportunities and expecting good results, "lucky people" are more successful. They are also used to being offered these opportunities and are prepared to work on them. They learn more new things and are curious and excited about all life has to offer. That preparation also makes them seem luckier since "it always works out for them."

All of this because they are positive, expect success, and are prepared. They are "lucky".

And "lucky" people are happier people.

So make your own luck.

>> Be positive

>> Expect the best

>> Be prepared to take advantage of opportunities

Don't believe in Luck -- believe in YOURSELF!

Do You Believe in Luck? - Bullet Points

This is your chance to create bullet points from the readings about incredible people. We have done the first one for you.

- Are some people more lucky?

- Scientists have shown that people's "luck" is all the same

- People who think they are lucky have a positive outlook on life

- People who see themselves as lucky get more opportunities given to them because they are positive

- Because they expect the best and get more opportunities, they are more successful

- To be lucky yourself, be positive, expect to succeed, and prepare well to take advantage of new opportunities

- Believe in yourself and you will be successful

Emotional Intelligence

	SELF	SOCIAL
RECOGNITION — Who I am (Awareness)	**Self Awareness** — being able to recognize and understand your own emotions	**Social Awareness** — being able to recognize and understand someone else's emotions and empathize with those emotions
REGULATION — What I do (Regulation)	**Self Management** — the ability to control or alter your impulses and make decisions based on thought with emotion rather than emotion alone	**Social Skills** — the ability to to manage relationships based on your own self-awareness, self-management and social awareness

What is Emotional Intelligence?

Emotional intelligence (EQ) is the ability to identify, use, understand, and manage emotions in positive ways to relieve stress, communicate effectively, empathize with others, overcome challenges, and defuse conflict.

Lots of big words. But what does it mean and what does it do for you?

> EQ is the skill you use to:
> - recognize and control your emotions.
> - recognize other people's emotions and get along with them.

Emotional Intelligence lets you:

Know yourself and your emotions

    a. Recognize and understand what you are feeling

    b. Recognize and understand why you are feeling this way

    c. Recognize and understand the causes of those feelings

Manage your emotions and yourself

    a. Recognize the early signs of unwanted emotions

    b. Control unwanted emotions

    c. Learn how to lessen and quickly change unwanted emotions into positive emotions.

Know others

    a. Recognize and understand what others are feeling

    b. Recognize and understand why others are feeling this way

    c. Recognize and understand the causes of those feelings by empathizing with others

Manage relationships

    a. Use the ability to recognize emotions in others to empathize with them

    b. Use the ability to recognize emotions in others to better deal with them during stressful situations

    c. Use the ability to recognize emotions to better lead and motivate others through empathy

Why do I need to be Emotionally Intelligent?

- You will make better decisions by balancing emotion and thought
- Lower stress levels and sleep better
- Do better in school by being able to focus more
- Have better and closer relationships with friends, family, and teachers
- Be healthier – fewer colds and flus
- Less anxiety and more positive outlook on life
- Express yourself better
- Easier to achieve your goals
- Better negotiation skills – more likely to have WIN-WIN negotiations and get what you need
- Not be overwhelmed by emotions and mood swings
- Resolve conflicts positively without violence
- Find solutions to challenges faster

Can I really be more Emotionally Intelligent?

You aren't born with Emotional Intelligence.

Everything you know about emotions you have learned.

We will be doing many exercises to help you increase your emotional intelligence and participating in those activities will strengthen your EQ skills.

There is a secret weapon to expanding your EQ skills that will also propel you to success in all areas of your life.

Self-Discipline – Creating Your Own Plan

First, you need a goal – something you want to become a habit – even if it is just for a short time. That might be finishing your homework, always studying a week for before a test, or not stopping my homework just because my favorite show is on.

Now find a trigger (the IF part of the plan). This might be a time (bedtime), a situation (Sabre-Tooth Tiger), or a feeling (hungry).

Now what are you going to do when that IF thing happens? That is the THEN part of the plan (sleep, run, eat).

GOAL
Study for my test every night for a week.

IF
8 pm

THEN
study for 20 min

IF-THEN STATEMENT:
If I have a test within the next week, then I will study at 8 pm every night for 20 minutes.

Do you have the self-discipline to make AND KEEP your plans?

my IF - THEN Plan

GOAL

IF

THEN

IF-THEN STATEMENT:

GOAL

IF

THEN

IF-THEN STATEMENT:

What is an Investment?

Do you like money?

OK, that's a trick question. We all like money and we all would like to have enough money to be comfortable, buy the things we want, travel, etc.

As you get older, you will make more money (hopefully) as you go from job to job, career to career. If you are like most people, each time you get a raise (your job pays you more money each week), you will spend more money. You might buy a nicer car, you might buy a bigger house, and take a vacation.

If you were paying attention earlier, you will also be investing more. Remember the 70-10-10-10 rule? You can't spend all your raise, you have to break it into each of the groups, including investments.

Some Financial Words

To learn about investing, we need to learn some financial vocabulary.

In accounting, you have assets and liabilities. An asset is something that has a value and can help you pay off debts. An asset could be your bank account or your investments. A liability is something that you owe. A liability could be a loan, a mortgage, or your credit card.

Assets are good!

Liabilities are bad.

Investments

An investment is something you put money into with the goal of making even more money from it. You are putting money into something now to get future benefits — usually long into the future (like for your retirement). For example, you could buy stocks on the stock market. Each month, you would buy more stocks to increase your portfolio (the value of the stocks you own). You buy stocks at a low price and the value of those stocks hopefully will grow. If the value seems to have peaked, you might sell that stock, getting back your original amount plus a profit. For a true investment, you would then turn all that money into another investment. No spending your profits from your investments.

True Assets as Investments

Although your banker would see your house as an asset, we are going give a narrower definition of an asset. For us, an investment asset is something that, even if you don't put any more money into it, your investment will continue to grow. If you bought stocks, and then stopped buying more stocks, your original investment would still be there and grow. However, if you stopped paying the mortgage on your house, they would take back your house and you lose your investment.

Grow Your Investments

The goal is to find investments that grow over time. There are many types of investments that we will discuss in Part 2. For now, an investment is something that will keep growing even if you don't put any more money into it.

Monthly Goal

What is your Goal?

Specific-Measurable -Actionalble-Risky-Timed-Exciting-Relavent

Why Do You Want This Goal?

What Are Your Obstacles?

What Knowledge Do You Need?

Who Can Help You?

What Is Your Plan?

Now use this information to create your success plan!

_____
_____
_____
_____
_____
_____
_____
_____
_____
_____
_____

See yourself already successful.
Feel what it will be like to have succeeded.
Think about how good you will feel
several times per day.

Never Give Up

Memory

Why is Memory Important?

Memory can help you:

- Spend less time studying
- Easier to take tests & higher marks
- Higher self-esteem
- Keeps you organized and on time
- You will be promoted sooner and get higher pay at work
- Remember jokes to tell your friends
- Remember people's names
- You will have less stress for the rest of your life

But I don't have a good memory

Memory is not genetic. Anyone can have a good memory. It just takes training practice.

> You increase your memory ability by using 3 "tricks":
>
> Association - linking what you want to remember with something easier to remember
>
> Location - when we try to remember something (like what we did yesterday), we usually try to remember where we were first
>
> Imagination - makes the associations more memorable

Practice

Good Memory is like any other skill — it gets better with practice.

Over the next few pages, you will see some strategies for good memory skills.

You might have seen them before but that is because they work so well, we want to make sure you know them well. The more you practice, the better your memory will become.

> You might even become as good as the current record holder, David Farrow, who can remember the random order of 59 packs of playing cards with only 1 mistake!

Basic Rules of Memory

To have an effective, trained memory, follow these rules:

Try to be Interested
    a. Sometimes it is hard to be interested in a subject but the harder you try to find a connection with your own life, the easier it will be to remember things.

Understand it
    a. If you understand something, it is easier to remember it.

    b. If you know the area of a triangle (Base X Height/2) is that way because it is half of a rectangle, the formula makes sense and is more memorable.

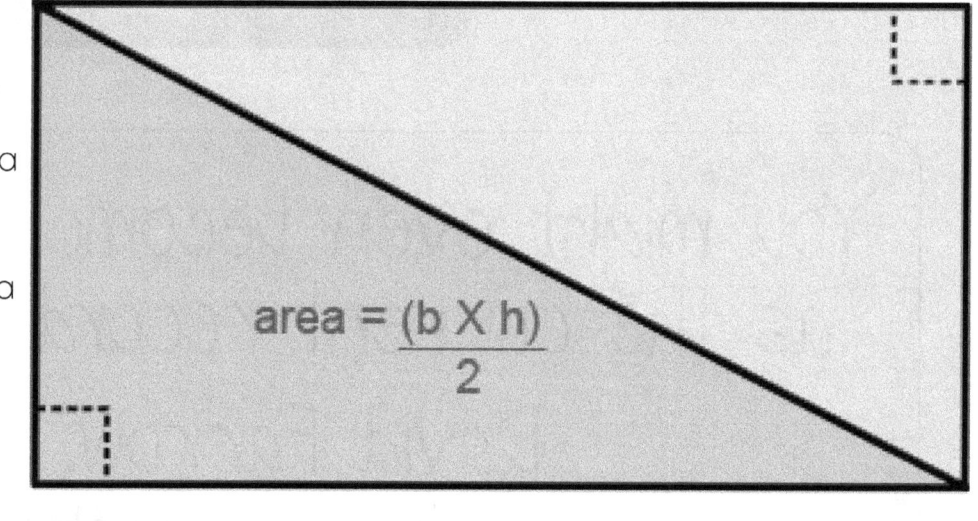

Have confidence in your memory
    a. Don't use the excuse that you have a bad memory. Everyone can have a good memory, it just takes practice, focus, and some "tricks".

Pay Attention

a. You aren't going to remember what you don't hear or see — so pay attention.

b. Listen to your teacher and focus on what is being said.

c. When someone tells you their name, actually listen to it and use it in conversation a couple times. Repeating it aloud will help.

d. When you set something down (book, keys, phone, etc.) pay attention to where you put them. If you set them down when you are thinking of something else, you will forget.

e. When you are trying to remember something, eliminate distractions like phones or papers.

Review and Overlearn

a. After you learn something new, review it as soon as possible.

b. Edit your notes with additional information.

c. Quiz yourself rather than just re-reading notes. Memory is like a muscle, a bit of strain will develop it. Force yourself to have to remember it.

Talk Out Loud

a. When you review your notes and school work, talk out loud.

b. This triggers learning from sight and sound.

Visualization Tips
For Making Things More Memorable

Exaggeration
a. Make everything different and strange in your visualizations.
b. Use size, weight, etc. to exaggerate your image.
c. If you are using a monkey in your visualization, use a gorilla instead.
d. Make things too big or too small.

Be ridiculous
a. You need to remember bananas. Don't have a monkey hold the banana, use a gorilla.
b. Don't just make it a gorilla, make it King Kong on top of the Empire State Building.

Lots of color
a. Always use bright colours in your visualization.
b. Use colour to make it more ridiculous — a purple King Kong.

Movement
a. Make your visualizations move and interact.
b. Have a cowboy in your visualization? Make him swing a lasso and rope whatever you are trying to remember.

Use all your senses
a. Use smell/touch/sound/taste as well as visual cues.

Visualization Tips

Your turn to make your things MEMORABLE!

Start with an object (like we did with the monkey) and add to it.

> **Starting object**

Exaggeration

Be ridiculous

Lots of color

Movement

Use all your senses

Self-Discipline Week

This week you will practice Self-Discipline by working on a habit that will help you. Actions or activities normally take about 60 days of practice to become a true habit.

Can you make it through one week practicing a new good habit?

I will practice self-discipline by:

What Did You Learn About Yourself

What was easy about your week?

What was difficult about your week?

What will you do different to be more successful?

Effective Speaking

Nervous?

Public speaking can be a very scary thing. Most adults are afraid to speak in front of even a small group of people. With practice, preparation, and a confident attitude, you can become an excellent speaker. You will be able to speak in front of any size group.

It Is All The Same

Whether you speak in front of one person, 10 people, 100 people, or 1,000 people, it is all the same. Whether you are talking at the dinner table, telling your friend a joke or delivering a speech to an auditorium of people, you are doing the EXACT same thing. You have been doing public speaking for years now. The size of the audience is the only difference and that difference doesn't matter.

On the following pages are some tips to be an effective speaker. Then, you have some space to create 6 short speeches.

The speech should be 1-2 minutes long about a topic that you pick. Please keep the topic appropriate for school and your audience. These short speeches will help you gain experience and confidence to be able to speak in any situation.

Where Will You Use Effective Speaking

Being comfortable speaking in any situation will help you with:

- School Presentations
- Assemblies
- Job Interviews
- University Interviews
- Applying for loans/mortgages
- Negotiating purchases
- Toasts at Weddings/Birthday Parties
- Funerals and Memorials
- Sales Meetings
- Board Meetings
- Talking to customers
- Meeting new people
- Persuading people
- Confidence
- Self-Esteem

How To Be An Effective Speaker

To be an effective speaker, there are several things you can do to improve your performance. And yes, it is a performance so you will be practicing using logic, drama, vocal techniques, and good grammar. With practice, you will soon find speaking to a group can be fun!

Be prepared

Make sure that you spend time polishing your speech. Then make sure you know it well. Practice your speech many times before you have to give it. Practicing your speech and knowing your material will give you confidence and reduce your anxiety.

Use the Memory Palace

Effective speaking is not reading. You do not want to read your speech, you want to deliver it. That means it should be committed to memory as much as possible. Use your memory techniques to learn your speech.

Use Personal Stories

Bring your audience with you on the journey that is your speech. Insert a personal story, if it goes along with the topic of your speech. And you don't have to make yourself look good. If you show a failure you have had and how you recovered and carried on, your audience will be behind you.

Relax Yourself Before You Begin

Use some breathing exercise and meditation to relax yourself. Before you go up to do your speech relax your shoulders and neck.

Fake That Smile

Before you go on stage, put a pencil lengthwise between your teeth and bite down for 1 minute. This activity simulates smiling and has been proven to elevate your mood.

Use Good Posture

Stand straight and proud. You don't have to be stiff but keep your shoulders square and your posture upright. Slouching shows fear and uncertainty.

Use Your Body & Your Hands

You want good posture but don't be afraid to use your body and gesture with your hands. Be expressive with your hand gestures but don't overdo it. Practice your hand gestures to go along with your speech. This may sound backwards but practicing your hand gestures will actually make them seem natural and unrehearsed.

Use humor

Don't be afraid to use a little bit of humor. But don't try to be a stand-up comedian if that is not the real you. Be you.

Know your audience

Remember who you are speaking to and speak their language. Don't try to look smart by using big words.

Smile

You faked the smile before the speech, now do it for real. Your audience will be more accepting if you are smiling.

Keep Eye Contact

Look at your audience and maintain some eye contact. Your audience will pay attention more if look at them. This is why you have to be prepared, so you don't have to read your notes while you talk.

Slow Down

You will want to speak quickly to get it over with. Try to slow down. Use pauses to highlight some of your points.

Use Your Voice

Change the pitch (lower, higher), volume (up, down), and speed (faster, slower) of your voice as you deliver your speech. Emphasize important words to go along with your hand gestures.

Have Fun

Speaking in front of groups can be lots of fun. The more you do it, the better you will become. Relax and enjoy yourself. Entertain, inform, and win over your audience.

Sample Speech Topics

For practice, you should do at a 1-2 minute speech every month in front of your class. As you do more speeches, you will become more comfortable and confident speaking in front of groups.

On the following pages is an area to brainstorm your topic and write down some notes.

Here are some sample topics for a speech or come up with your own.

My biggest concern for the future is...	Intelligence is not enough.
Real wealth is never measured in money or possessions.	If I ruled the world...
Conservation is survival.	Color affects the way people feel.
If I were an animal I'd be a...	Team sports build strong individuals.
Plants have feelings too.	Laughter is the best medicine.
Junk food's popularity relies on marketing.	Fools and their money are easily parted.
To err is human. To forgive is divine.	Self-Discipline is not a dirty word.
The world is a smaller place these days.	Beauty is in the eye of the beholder.
The more we communicate, the less we really say.	Children learn what they live with.
When I grow up...	What characteristics make an ideal hero and why?
Goals are good for you.	What and who is an average person?
Have I told you about my pet?	Being young is over-rated.
	The most important lesson of my life so far...

To know your emotions, you should learn the physical reaction for each. List 3 physical reactions you have to:

Anger

Frustration

Fear

Shame

Sadness

What is meditation?

Meditation is awareness.

This awareness can take many different forms either through focus or visualization. Meditation results in a calming of the mind, helping to reduce the number of scattered thoughts that we all have all day.

How Can Meditation Help?

Meditation has many varied benefits.

It calms the mind and reduces stress.

- clearer thoughts
- better focus and concentration
- better grades
- easier to learn
- be more creative
- help control your emotions
- increases memory
- increase positive attitude
- reduce fear, depression, and anxiety
- increase self-esteem, confidence, self-image

How To Meditate

Meditation is the calming of the mind and this can be done anywhere.

Your goal should be to reach a meditative state, a state of calm and relaxation, in the middle of a tornado. You need meditation most when everything around you seems to be spinning out of control.

However, to begin it is better to start in a quiet room.

Find your space

Find a quiet room and get comfortable. You don't have to be in any special position (like cross legged on the floor). You can be sitting, lying down, or have your head resting on your desk. Sitting up is easiest for the breathing exercises. It is easier to block out the world if you close your eyes but that is not necessary.

Breathe

Begin by breathing. You might be thinking that we are starting really easy here but good breathing takes practice. Breathe

in slowly, holding your breath for a count of 4 and then breathe out. Keep breathing in this regular, slow method. Keep breathing in the same regular rhythm as you continue the rest of your meditation.

Once you have done this for a moment, relax your body. Let go of all the muscles. Don't wiggle or move, just let them all go slack and feel the breathing take away the negative energy every time you breathe out and bring in the good energy every time you breathe in. Imagine the waves of the ocean going in and out as you continue to breathe and relax.

Focus

Continue breathing and let yourself focus on the thought of the day. Your thought of the day can be anything. Possibly, you want to solve a challenge — focus on the joy you will feel when you have solved the

challenge. Do not focus on the challenge but rather the joy of having found a solution. Convince your body that you have found a solution.

Now, focus on what you will take away from your meditation — something that will stay with you for the rest of the day. This might be a particular strength or virtue you want to take away with you — clarity of thought, confidence, thankfulness.

Positive Energy Flow

Now let the thoughts drift away from you as you once again start your breathing exercises. Focus your thoughts on the positive energy flowing into your body. Let the calmness and relaxation flow through your body.

Slowly open your eyes and enjoy your calm, relaxed nature. Keep your strength with you all day by recalling it simply by taking 3 deep breaths.

Who meditates?

Some of the most successful people in the world meditate

The list of people who meditate is long and includes the biggest names from movies, television, music, sports, fashion, and even billionaire business people.

Kendrick Lamar - Rapper

Hugh Jackman - actor, Broadway star

Derek Jeters - athlete

Ophray Winfrey - television, magazine, billionaire

Lady Gaga - singer

Demi Lovato - singer

Beyonce - singer, songwriter, actress

Kobe Bryant - athlete

Will Smith - actor, rapper, producer

Johnathan Van Ness - television personality

Arianna Huffington - billionaire business woman

Danai Gurira - actress

Mayiam Bialik - actress

Cristiano Ronaldo - athlete

Law of Belief

What is the Law?

The Law of Belief states that whatever you believe, with feeling, will happen.

How Does it work?

We create our own lives with our beliefs. What you believe with confidence will become your reality. Negative beliefs can make you hit a wall.

We all have limiting beliefs that convince us that we can't do something. A limiting belief is something you think about yourself that prevents you from being as successful as you could be.

Because we believe we can't do it, or believe something is going to go wrong, we will fail. If we believe we can achieve something, you are more likely to be successful.

If you believe you can do something or believe you can't, you are correct. STOP your limiting beliefs.

How Can I make the Law of Belief work for me?

The best way to make the Law of Belief work for you is look at what you believe about yourself. Find the things that are stopping you from being successful.

What aren't you trying because you "believe" you won't be successful?

Where does that belief come from? Did you fail once and then give up?

Instead, believe that you can do anything that you set your mind to achieve.

Don't limit yourself by your own beliefs. Use your Success Log to realize how much of a success you can be.

Think positive and believe in yourself.

Example of the Law of Belief

Start every day believing that wonderful things are going to happen to you.

Make your affirmation be:

> I can do and be anything I set my mind to!

See Your True Self

What do you see?

When you look at yourself, what do you see?

Are you seeing a loser or a winner? Do you see someone who is smart or stupid?

True or False?

You see someone who is a loser, but your friends see a winner.

They are just "being nice". They don't know the truth, but YOU do!

Do we know the TRUTH?

We know what the TRUTH is, don't we? What we see is our reality. We make our own reality with what what we perceive. So, all we have to do is change how we see ourselves to change our reality.

How do you see yourself?

What three words describe how you see yourself?

_____

_____

_____

How do you feel about yourself?

What three words describe how you feel about yourself?

_____

_____

_____

Are these beliefs right or wrong?

Why are these beliefs right or wrong?

_____

_____

_____

Only positive beliefs now!

What three words describe your good qualities? (Yes, you do have them.)

_____

_____

_____

Prepare a 1-2 minute speech to deliver to your class:

Speech topic

Brainstorming (use your brainstorming skills)

My Speech

Self-Discipline Week

This week you will practice Self-Discipline by working on a habit that will help you. Actions or activities normally take about 30 days of practice to become a true habit.

Can you make it through one week practicing a new good habit?

I will practice self-discipline by:

What Did You Learn About Yourself

What was easy about your week?

What was difficult about your week?

What will you do different to be more successful?

Control Your Anger

We all get angry. Whether we lost the big game, we didn't get what we wanted from our parents, or our brother or sister broke our favourite toy. We all have ways to deal with anger — some are good, and some are bad.

Now is your chance to use your brainstorming skills to come up with a list of things you can do in reaction to anger. List all the ways, good and bad, that we might use (like kicking things, counting to 10, hitting your brother). Then circle the ones you think are useful reactions.

_____   _____
_____   _____
_____   _____
_____   _____
_____   _____
_____   _____
_____   _____
_____   _____
_____   _____
_____   _____

How To Take A Test

General Information for all types of tests

You have already reviewed your study notes and looked over previous tests to see where you might have done a better job. Now it is test day.

No matter what type of test you are going to take, you should follow certain steps immediately before the test.

Arrive early.

a. Make sure you arrive early to the test.

b. Arriving early means you have everything you will need for the test (pens, pencils, rulers, protractor, calculator, etc.) so you aren't stressed about forgetting something.

Meditation

a. Because you are early and prepared, you have time to use your meditation techniques to calm and focus your mind.

Review

a. When you get the test, do a quick overview of the test so you have an idea of what to expect.

b. Look over the value of questions to be sure you give yourself enough time for the bigger questions.

Read Carefully

a. Many mistakes are made because students don't read the question carefully and end up giving the wrong answer or an incomplete answer.

Be strategic in answering questions

a. Answer the easy questions first to build your confidence.

b. Then, answer the higher mark questions so you maximize your results.

Review

a. If you have time at the end, look over the test (particularly the higher value questions).

b. Check for:
- spelling and grammar
- math calculations
- incomplete answers

> Do your best and be proud of yourself!

Monthly Goal

What is your Goal?

Specific-Measurable -Actionalble-Risky-Timed-Exciting-Relavent

Why Do You Want This Goal?

What Are Your Obstacles?

What Knowledge Do You Need?

Who Can Help You?

What Is Your Plan?

Now use this information to create your success plan!

See yourself already successful.
Feel what it will be like to have succeeded.
Think about how good you will feel
several times per day.

Never Give Up

True Cost of Borrowing

You are practicing self-discipline each day. One of the most important ways to practice self-discipline is in how you spend your money. Using the 10-10-10-70 rule and budgeting to live on 70% of what you earn will lead to massive financial success. Right now, that likely means maybe just your allowance and presents that you receive. Keep that up and that means you can get rich.

But self-discipline is REALLY HARD. We want everything faster than it takes to heat a Pizza Pocket in the microwave. We see something, we must buy it right away — even when we don't have the money.

People do not have self-discipline. Today, most people don't just spend 100% of what they earn (instead of just 70%) they spend even more than they earn.

Huh? They spend more than they earn? How can they do that? The simple answer is something called CREDIT.

What is Credit?

Credit is when you buy something (car, house, vacation, groceries, dinner out, a pair of shoes) and promise to pay for it later. You get what you want now (even if you don't have the money) and get to pay for it in a week, a year, 10 years.

How cool is that? Get what you want now and then pay for it later. You use someone else's (usually a bank or a credit card company's) money to get what you want.

What's The Catch?

When something is too good to be true, it usually isn't true. There is a catch.

You also must pay something called interest. Interest is the fee you pay for using the other person's money. That can get expensive. At some of the highest rates, something that is $100 that you wait a year to pay back can cost you $133.20. A lack of self-discipline just cost you $33.20.

You and your friend want to take a 1-week vacation to Disney World that costs $10,000. You save for two years at 5% interest and your friend puts it on his credit card at 18% interest. You both have $400 per month in your budget for the vacation.

You save for 2 years and because of compound interest only pay $9,600 for the $10,000 vacation.

Your friend does go on vacation sooner. However, also because of compound interest, they take two years and 8 months to pay it back and their $10,000 vacation actually costs $12,628.

However, you are way more motivated to put the $400 away than your friend is to pay the $400. They already have the reward. What if they decide to pay only $350 per month? It now takes 3 years and 2 months and ends up costing $13,156. For that amount, they could have stayed for 2 more nights!

You must remember to always look at the TRUE cost of borrowing.

The True Picture

The "Bad Luck" of Soichrio Honda

Even the most successful businesses have to begin somewhere.

Even the most successful businesspeople have "Bad Luck."

When Soichiro Honda started, he had one goal – to sell his newly invented piston assembly to Toyota. He used all his savings and even sold his wife's jewellery to finance a machine shop. When he sent his finished product to Toyota, they said it wasn't good enough. He had to return to school – and the laughter of his classmates and teachers.

Honda had perseverance – he kept working on his idea. He lived in his machine shop and finally convinced Toyota. However, Japan was preparing for war and Honda couldn't get the cement he needed for his factory. Honda used his innovation and his team developed a way to create the concrete he needed!

Honda finally had success – except his factory was bombed twice and he wouldn't get the raw materials he needed. Again, Honda persevered by having his workers go out and collect the metal gas canisters that the American fighter pilots dropped. He used these for the raw materials. Still disaster plagued Honda. An earthquake destroyed his factory and he had to sell everything to Toyota.

Broke and faced with a gas shortage in post-war Japan, Honda couldn't drive his car to get food. He used his innovation to create a motor for his bicycle. Soon all his neighbours wanted one. Honda quickly ran out of motors. He realized he needed another factory but had no money.

That wasn't enough to stop Honda. He wrote to the bicycle manufacturers in Japan by hand (no computers back then). 5,000 of them could see his vision and Honda was again in business. Yet, his motorized bike still didn't sell well because it was too big and bulky. Honda saw what was needed and made more innovative adjustments. His new, smaller bike was a hit. He even won an award from the Emperor of Japan.

Honda has since gone on to sell his motorcycles and cars to the rest of the world. His company is the second best selling Japanese car manufacturer in the world.

Honda failed over and over. "Bad Luck" and negative forces worked against him. Most people would have given up their dream in the face of these problems. Honda proved that perseverance, creativity, and hard work is the road to success.

The "Bad Luck" of Soichrio Honda - Bullet Points
Create bullet points from the reading (answer on page 180).

Brainstorming

List Method

I bet you can guess how the List Method works. Yes, we make lists but there are some special rules involved that will make the job easier and make you even more successful.

The 5 Minute List

At the top of your paper, write your challenge in the form of a question.

> What could I do to help my team score more baskets in each game?

Now, set a timer for 5 minute and continue writing down ideas for 5 minutes. DON'T look at the timer, focus on the page.

Try hard to keep writing ideas constantly.

Write down all ideas no matter how crazy they might seem.

Even if you can't think of something, write down "I am full of great ideas" Until the next thought comes into your head. The idea is not to take the pencil off the paper.

At the end of 5 minutes, go over your list and see what you have. Pick your best ideas and begin to develop a plan around those ideas.

The 20 Item List

Make sure you have an hour of uninterrupted time for this method.

At the top of a lined sheet of paper, write your challenge in the form of a question.

> What could I do to help my team score more baskets in each game?

Now number your lines from 1 to 20.

Now write 20 ideas and do not stop until you have 20 actual ideas (even if they are a little crazy).

The first 5 to 8 ideas will come easily. The next 5-8 will be harder. The last 4-5 ideas will be very hard to come up with.

Usually, the best ideas will be in the numbers 15-20 because this is where you have stretched your creativity to the limit.

1.
2.
3.
4.
5.
6.
7.
8.
9.
10.
11.
12.
13.
14.
15.
16.
17.
18.
19.
20.

These methods can be used in groups as well.

If you are using the 5 minute method, have each person do their own list for 5 minutes and then share your ideas.

Use the 20 idea method as a group discussion. Have one person keep track of the ideas on a large sheet of paper or chalk board so everyone can see the ideas.

No Complaining Day

Today is the day that you will practice Self-Discipline by not complaining for a full day.

Complaining

Complaining focuses on what we don't want rather than what we want. A complaint is when we talk about what we want to change with someone who has no power to change it. Complaining does nothing constructive and works against you by constantly reminding you of the negative things in your life. Especially, when we complain to someone who can't do anything about your complaint.

Rather than focusing on the negative, take initiative, take control and work on the positive solution to your complaint. Calmly and respectfully discuss your complaint with someone with the ability and authority to make a change. And if there is nobody to solve the problem, focusing on finding the positive in the challenge.

Challenge

Challenge your friends and family to a No Complaining Day and help each other find the positives in everything.

My biggest 3 complaints are:

[   ]

The people I need to talk to that can help me with my complaints are:

[   ]

How did you feel at the end of the day?

[   ]

> Complaining is finding faults. Wisdom is finding solutions.

Confidence

Confidence is critical to your success, not only in school but in life.

If we are confident, we are ready for life and all the challenges and experiences that life offers to us. Even if we are not successful, confidence gives us the ability to try again. A lack of confidence can prevent people from reaching their full success.

Confidence is a trust in yourself. Confidence is trust in your own judgement, your ability, your skills, and your own capabilities.

Confidence – Competence Loop

Confidence and Competence go hand in hand. As your confidence grows, you take more chances, try new things, and keep trying even when you have some "failure" (remember you only fail when you give up). This determination builds your competence.

That new competence becomes a demonstration of your own capabilities which gives your confidence a boost. With more confidence, your competence increases and so goes the loop.

> Most important belief you can have:
>
> **I can solve any problem I am faced with.**

Take the Confidence test

How confident are you? Take this test and check your results on the next page.

Circle the number that agrees with how often you do each thing or how much you agree with the statement. For instance, do you ask for help? 1 means you never ask for help, 3 means you ask for help half of the time, 5 means you will always ask for help when you are stuck on a task.

	never	sometimes			usually
I ask for help when I am stuck on a task	1	2	3	4	5
I like the way I look	1	2	3	4	5
I am comfortable meeting new people	1	2	3	4	5
I accept criticism—without getting mad	1	2	3	4	5
I like to try new things—even the hard things	1	2	3	4	5
I am happy with myself	1	2	3	4	5
I set goals for myself	1	2	3	4	5
I like when good things happen to others	1	2	3	4	5
I am happy with my relationships	1	2	3	4	5
I keep trying no matter what	1	2	3	4	5

Add up all your answers to get your TOTAL _____

On the next page, see how you did and some ways you can increase your confidence.

Check your results

How confident are you? What were your results?

TOTAL SCORE:_____

41-50	Great confidence
31-40	Your confidence is above average
21-30	You lack some confidence
10-20	Your confidence needs serious work

Regardless of how you scored, you likely need work on your confidence. Here are some tips:

1) Look at what you have already achieved. That is what the Success Log is for.

2) Give yourself better self-talk. If you talk trash to yourself, you are never going to believe you are capable of great things.

3) Make a list of all the things you are good at to build your confidence for doing other things.

4) Assume the power pose. This is how Wonder Woman or Superman stand, hands on hips, legs spread should width. Standing this way for 2 minutes can actually increase your confidence before a test or game (backed by science).

5) Do the Right Thing. Confident people have a value system that defines the way they act and they live up to those values. Be the best version of yourself.

Self-Discipline Week

This week you will practice Self-Discipline by working on a habit that will help you. Actions or activities normally take about 30 days of practice to become a true habit.

Can you make it through one week practicing a new good habit?

I will practice self-discipline by:

What Did You Learn About Yourself

What was easy about your week?

What was difficult about your week?

What will you do different to be more successful?

Prepare a 1-2 minute speech to deliver to your class:

Speech topic

Brainstorming (use your brainstorming skills)

My Speech

How To Make Decisions

T-Chart Decision Analysis

Benjamin Franklin is famous for using this type of decision making model.

Be sure of the question

Clearly identify the decision to be made. Often, when making a decision, we are asking ourselves the wrong question.

You might be asking yourself:

Question #1 - Should I take a martial art?

Maybe you already know you <u>want</u> to take a martial art. A better question would be:

Question #2 - Should I take Karate or Aikido?

T Charts

T-Charts work well when it is a yes or no question such as Question #1. First, as with any decision, gather any information you might need to make the decision. Accurate knowledge is the key.

Write the question at the top of a sheet of paper. Divide the paper down the middle with a vertical line. On the left write PRO (YES) and on the right, write CON (NO).

List the reason why you should (Pro) and shouldn't (CON) make this choice and see which side is stronger.

Example for a Yes or No question

Should I take a martial art?

Pro
- defend myself
- get in shape
- meet new friends
- gain confidence
- better balance

Con
- takes time
- might get hurt
- costs money

Example for a Multi-choice question

Which Martial Art should I take?

Karate
- Pro
- Con

Aikido
- Pro
- Con

Do you have a Yes or No decision to make?

What is your question?

Now list your PROS & CONS

Pro (good decision)

Con (bad decision)

How To Create a Vision Board

What is a Vision Board?

A Vision Board is a group of pictures, images, and words that show what we want in the coming days, months, and years. A Vision Board is a constant reminder to keep our wants and desires in our mind all the time. A Vision Board shows our future, our best self, our accomplishments, and our desires (wants).

What we think about (what we focus on) is what we bring about. (Law of Attraction).

The positive images from the Vision Board increase success and achievement by keeping what we want in our mind.

Olympic and professional athletes have been using visualization for years to enhance their training.

The Vision Board focuses on the positive thought of abundance and having achieved our goal rather than on the negative focus of not having enough.

131

Brainstorming Your Vision Board

Use the brainstorming techniques you have learned in this course to think of some of the goals you have and the images you might want to achieve.

Use creativity to think of images.

- Do you want to be more self-disciplined in doing your homework? How about an image of you working on your homework or handing your completed homework into your teacher?
- Do you want to excel in your favorite sport? How about doing a pretend article from your local newspaper talking about how you scored the winning points for your team in the playoffs?
- Do you want an A+ in your math course? How about an image of a math test with your name on it and a big red A+ at the top?
- Can't wait to play that new video game? Cut out a picture of the game and put it on your board.

> Your board can have any images you want but make sure they are:
> 1) Positive
> 2) Show the goal already achieved
> 3) Focus on what you really want in life, your ideal future
> 4) Are visual and emotional

How Do You Want To Be A Better Person?

What can you do to make yourself a better person?

You can't change the world but you can make the world a better place by making a better you.

What Do You Want To Achieve?

Are there any subjects you want to ecell at?

Is there a big event coming up?

Do you want to score an extra 10 points in your next basketball game?

What Things Would You Like?

Yes, you are allowed to want to have "things" but who you become and what you achieve will make the difference in how easy it is to actually get these things.

How to Create a Vision Board

Now that you have brainstormed your goals and what images would best represent those goals, the next step is to create your vision board.

A <u>Vision</u> Board is all about <u>images</u>. Your mind responds to pictures more than words. So go out and find pictures and images that represent what you want in your life. You can get those pictures from the Internet or from magazines (make sure you get permission before you cut up someone else's magazine).

As much as possible, put yourself in the picture. You can use a free computer drawing program or just cut and paste your picture on the image.

You can use words but if you do, paint a picture with the words.

Examples:

> If you want to score more baskets, put up a picture of a ball just going through a basket.

> If you want to get a better mark in math, create a picture of the top of a math test with your name and use a red pen to put the mark you want right beside your name.

> If you want to do well in a speech contest, make up a pretend newspaper headline saying that you have won the local Effective Speaking contest.

> If you want to go to Paris, get a picture of the Eifel Tower and paste a picture of you at the base of the tower waving.

Brainstorming Your Vision Board
(Using The List Method)

How Do You Want To Be A Better Person?	What Can Represent This On Your Vision Board?

What Do You Want To Achieve?	What Can Represent This On Your Vision Board?

What Things Would You Like?	What Can Represent This On Your Vision Board?

How to Use Your Vision Board

Make sure that you look at your vision board at least twice a day. The more often you see it and let the inspirations fill your mind, the better.

Start your day by <u>looking</u> at and <u>feeling</u> the joy your Vision Board represents.

See the future it represents as already having happened and experience the emotions you will feel when your goal is realized. Emotion is important so try to experience the success every day.

Use affirmations to reinforce your visualizations. Say your affirmations aloud with feeling and belief while you look at your board.

See yourself living the future the Vision Board shows.

Feel the emotion the future the Vision Board shows.

Believe you have already achieved everything on your Vision Board.

Be grateful for everything that is and will be yours.

Make sure you look at your Vision Board every night before bed.

> See and feel the images!

Use this space to sketch your Vision Board

Monthly Goal

What is your Goal?

Specific-Measurable-Actionalble-Risky-Timed-Exciting-Relavent

Why Do You Want This Goal?

What Are Your Obstacles?

What Knowledge Do You Need?

Who Can Help You?

What Is Your Plan?

Now use this information to create your success plan!

_____
_____
_____
_____
_____
_____
_____
_____
_____
_____
_____

See yourself already successful.
Feel what it will be like to have succeeded.
Think about how good you will feel
several times per day.

Never Give Up

Buying A Car

Rich people drive USED cars!

What?

You're thinking: "If I was rich, I wouldn't buy a used car. I'm rich. I don't have to buy someone else's car.

Or you've heard someone say: "If you buy a used car, you are just buying someone else's problems."

But remember the difference between an asset and a liability?

An asset is something that keeps making money for you even if you stop putting money in.

A liability costs you money and might totally disappear if you stop putting money into it.

A car is not an investment, it is a liability. It might be necessary, but it is still a liability. Each year, a car loses more and more of its value. And it never loses value as fast as the day you drive it off the lot. The minute you drive off the car lot in your brand new car, the value of that car drops. In the first year, your car loses 15-20% of its value.

Let's go with only 15% depreciation. That means, a $40,000 car is worth $34,000 after the first year and less than $29,000 by end of the second year.

That means, if you get a 5 year loan to pay for your car, you are spending the first year giving them money you will never get back.

After the second or third year, the depreciation slows a bit and the car maintains its value more.

If you want to be rich, let someone else take the hit for the first 2 years of depreciation. You buy the car after that and, if you maintain it well, you will be able to sell it in 2 or 3 years with very little loss.

Be smart. Buy the used car from a dealer with a good reputation. Check the car out thoroughly. Get a good deal and you will be happier knowing you didn't waste money.

Rich people don't throw money away on shiny toys.

Be smart and make sure your money stays with you.

Prepare a 1-2 minute speech to deliver to your class:

Speech topic

Brainstorming (use your brainstorming skills)

My Speech

Brainstorming

Mind Map

A mind map is a visual representation of your thoughts. You are mapping out your thoughts.

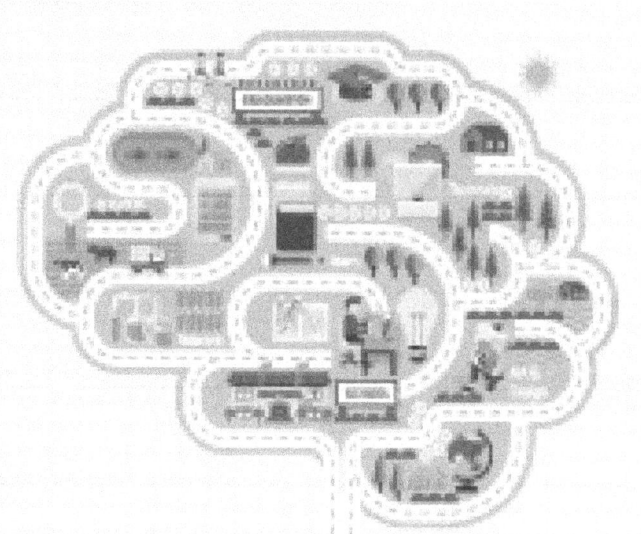

A mind map is especially useful for brainstorming essays and projects. Use mind maps during tests and exams for essay questions to answer the questions and organize our thoughts BEFORE you start writing your essay answer.

Mind maps can use words, pictures, numbers, and even colors.

Mind maps can also be used with many of the other brainstorming techniques.

Think of a mind map as a group of bicycle wheels. The center of the wheel is the main idea and then the spokes of the wheel stick out to other ideas or even more wheels. This way, ideas are grouped together for you and keep your thoughts organized.

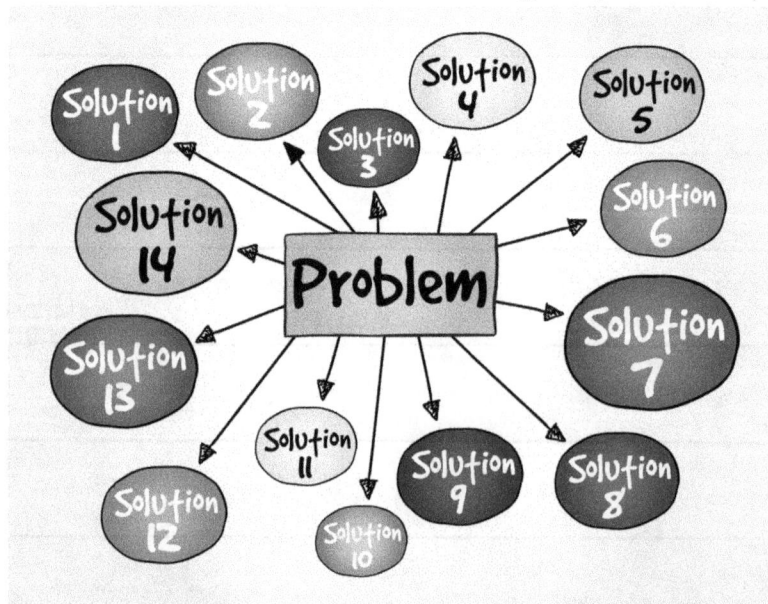

We have included an example of a mind map for a speech.

Start with a central idea – Power of Positive Thought.

Out from there, we have several other "Wheels" or secondary main thoughts.

My Story	Animatronics
Markiplier	Nothing is Impossible
My YouTube	Sign off from YouTube
Negative Thoughts	

There are spokes out from each of the secondary ideas. They give more and more detail about the idea.

Don't work on one spoke at a time. You are brainstorming and the ideas won't always come in a logical order. In fact, they won't come in a logical order. Just write them down.

Mind maps are very visual. If you are working on a big project and have several days to brainstorm, hang your mind map on the wall in your bedroom or put it in the first page of your binder so it is in front of your all the time. Add to it as ideas come to you.

And write the ideas down as soon as you think of them. You might think it is an amazing idea that you will never forget but that isn't how your brain works. Scientists have shown you will forget the new idea within 37 seconds if you don't act on it in some way.

Don't lose your idea; write it down in your journal. You do have a journal, right? Remember, you can use pictures, drawings, or anything else your mind can think of.

Mind Map Example

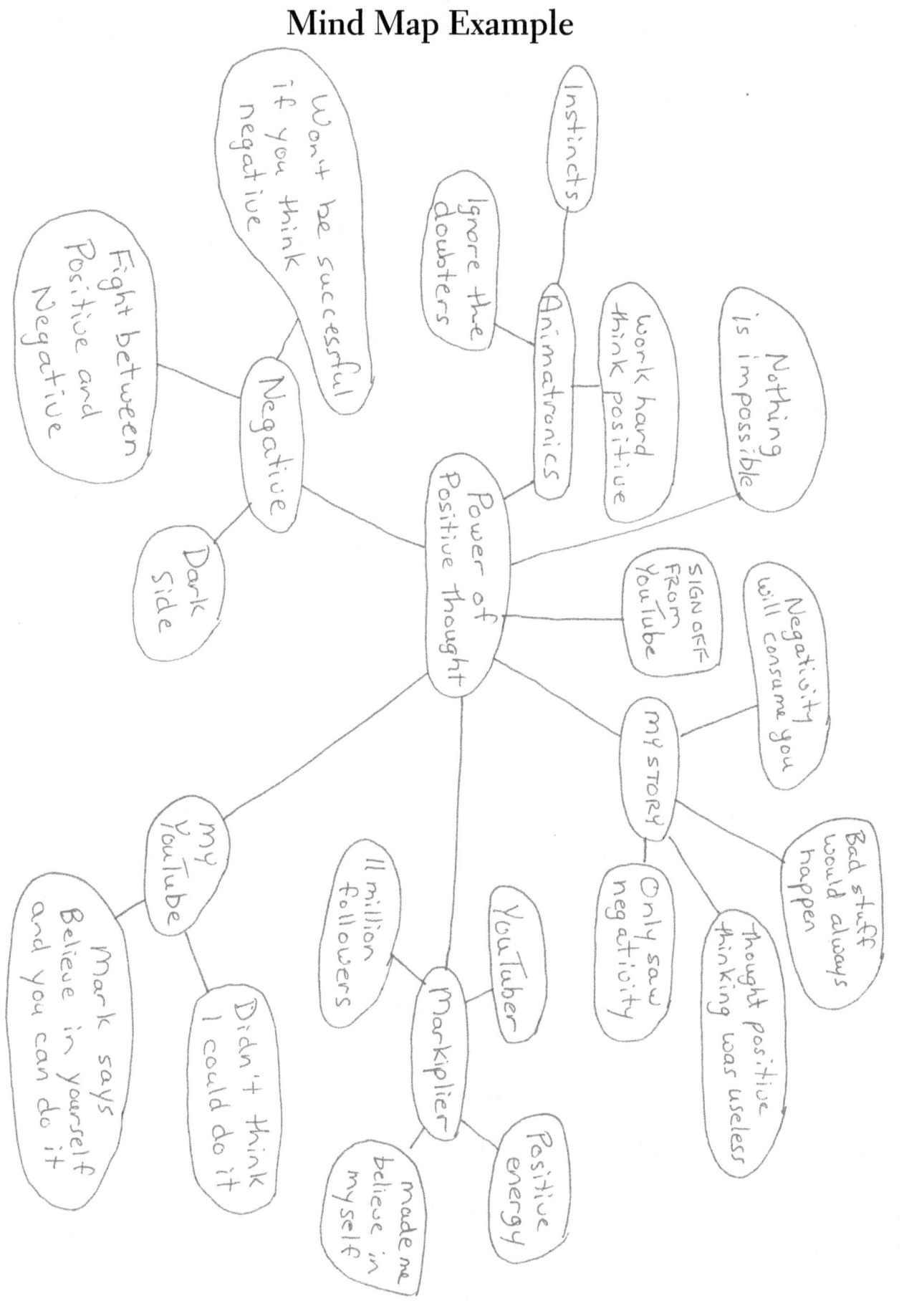

Sample speech
from Mind Map Brainstorming Example

Power of Positive Thought

Have any of you ever been so excited about something you want to do only to have someone tell you it is impossible! Well, I am here to tell you nothing is impossible.

If you don't try negativity will consume you. It will use you. Then it will dominate your life. Believe me. I have done the same thing before and it wasn't good.

I used to think very negatively. I would get up in the morning and my first thought would be what's going to go wrong today? I would expect all the bad stuff to happen to me. People would tell me to be positive and I would say, what is the sense of being positive? THAT'S NOT GOING TO DO ANYTHING. I just know something will go wrong today. All I saw was the negativity that surrounded me. I didn't believe in myself. I gave up easily. I didn't try at school. I cried a lot. I felt like I could not do anything right at all! Everything was impossible.

Until one day I got lucky. Has anyone here ever heard of a You tuber named Markiplier? From the very moment I found Mark on You Tube I knew my life was about to change. As I watched his video his words seems so powerful. He started to change the way I was thinking and feeling.

Mark says that we need to believe in ourselves. We need to be kind to other people and be a part of a community.

His energy is so positive you can't help but be positive just listening to him.

Mark is such an inspirational person that I want to be just like him. I KNOW THAT WE CAN ALL BE JUST LIKE HIM. Positive.

Mark believes in himself so much and is so positive that I saw Mark do the impossible. He got over 11 million followers on his You Tube channel. How is that for positivity?

The reason why I brought Markiplier up is because he not only helped change the way I was thinking and feeling, he also inspired me. As some of you may know I have a YouTube channel. The thing is I was afraid to have a YouTube channel before because

I didn't believe in myself until I heard what Mark always says in his videos which is

If you believe in yourself then you can do anything you want to do.

If you are thinking negatively than you are going to the dark side. What you should do with that negativity is not let it in but push it out of your head and forget it even exists. It's like a fight between the two sides that either positivity or negativity could win. In fact both of those sides are growing as we speak. What we want to do is stop the negativity from growing and let the positivity win the battle. There are so many things I want to do that I would not be able to do if I were thinking negative.

For example I was inspired to make some animatronics because of a game called Five Nights at Freddy's.

I was getting ready to build them but I want to make them interactive. Someone told me that THERE IS NO WAY I CAN GET THEM TO BE INTERACTIVE. I was so disappointed to think I couldn't do it. But Instead of listening to them I believed in myself and knew that I was at least going to give it a try. I decided to say, you know what, I am just going to pretend I didn't hear you say that and go on with my idea. The reason I said that is because I know I can do it and I know that because I am thinking positively.

Maybe you may have some things you want to try to do but you know they are going to be very difficult to pull off. Don't let people discourage you with their negativity.

YES some people ARE GOING TO SAY THAT THERE IS NO WAY YOU ARE GOING TO DO IT. YOU SHOULD JUST FORGET IT. I wouldn't listen to those people if I were you. If you really have a burning passion to do it and you know you're going to give it your all then don't let anything stop you.

You guys may not know how to do it but the answer is out there. Your instincts will sometimes kick in and tell you what the right thing to do is. Most of the time they will tell you to continue on with your idea and not give up. It is the same thing with the game I want to make, my u tube channel it is the same with everything you could possibly do in your life. All you have to do is think positive. Nothing can stop you. I know I have said it many times though out this speech, but I have said it so many times because it is true.

There will be difficult things in your life but I know for a fact you can get passed them. Nothing goes according to plan but with the power of positive thought it is never a mistake rather it is a way to learn and move on.

Work hard and think positive, those are my standards but they should be our standards.

    I thought I could pass that on to you.

So I have rambled on enough about the power of positive thought. Remember work hard and stay positive.

As I now say at the end of all my videos:

So until next time I will see you guys later

Positive Day
(Focus on what you want)

We are what we think about.

If you think about negative things, your focus will bring them into your life. If you think about what you want, you are more likely to bring those things into your life.

Our mood and our thoughts create how our day goes.

We create what we think about

Today is for thinking about what you want, not what you don't want.

As soon as you think, "I am going to fail that test", switch your thoughts to "I am prepared and I am going to get my best mark ever on that test". Of course, you must have been proactive and actually studied. Wishing won't make things happen — YOU make things happen!

Focus completely on what you want all day for one day. Be positive and eliminate negative thoughts.

Maybe you can make the same thing happen tomorrow too!

5 things I would really like and I will think about today are:

After the day is done, how did you do today?
How could you focus every day on what you want?

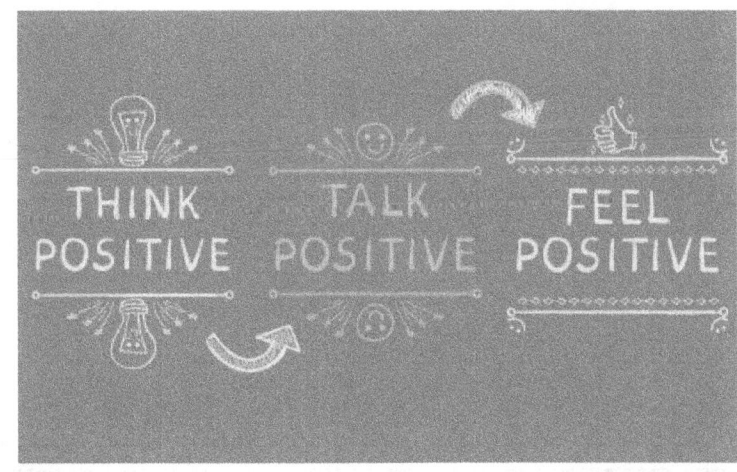

Prepare a 1-2 minute speech to deliver to your class:

Speech topic

Brainstorming (use your brainstorming skills)

My Speech

Law of Expectation

What is the Law?

The Law of Expectation states, we don't get what we want, we get what we expect.

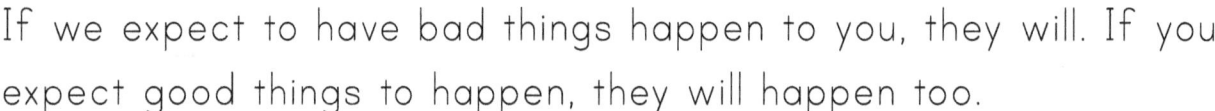

How Does it work?

Whatever you expect, with confidence, to happen will happen.

If we expect to have bad things happen to you, they will. If you expect good things to happen, they will happen too.

Is it any wonder things go wrong if you spend your time saying:

> Things never work out for me
>
> I never win at this
>
> I'm not going to pass this test

How Can I make it work for me?

Make your motto be "Wonderful things are happening to me!"

Always expect the best. Expect to get a good mark on your test. Expect that you will do well on your speech. Expect the best and it will happen.

Imagine that the universe is conspiring to make you happy.

Replace	With
I'll never win.	I always win
I won't make the shot	I will score
I am going to fail	I am successful
My life is terrible	Wonderful things are happening to me

Example

Think positive and positive things are more likely to happen to you.

Imagine that you can give that speech. Focus on you saying your speech perfectly and listening to all the applause. Expect to do well on your speech and focus on remembering all your speech perfectly.

And then, practice, practice, practice. Convince yourself that you expect to do well and then prove it by working hard to be the best you can be.

Remember

Remember wishes are just like air — they have no strength to them without positive action. Just expecting things to happen is not enough if you don't work hard and always keep trying.

What Expectations are you going to change?

Replace: **With:**

Self-Discipline Week

This week you will practice Self-Discipline by working on a habit that will help you. Actions or activities normally take about 30 days of practice to become a true habit.

Can you make it through one week practicing a new good habit?

Use the Habit Tracker at the end of the workbook.

I will practice self-discipline by:

What Did You Learn About Yourself

What was easy about your week?

What was difficult about your week?

What will you do different to be more successful?

How To Take A Test

Multiple Choice

> A shape with 3 sides is called a:
> A) Square
> B) Triangle
> C) Circle
> D) Rectangle

Read Carefully

a. Read the question carefully.

Answer yourself

a. Without looking at the answers, answer the question.

Check Your Answer

a. Now look at the answers.

b. Read all the answers to be sure.

All or None of the Above

a. You will see questions with "All of the Above" & "None of the Above" as one of the choices.

b. If one of the answers is <u>right</u> – eliminate None of the Above

c. If one of the answers is <u>wrong</u> – eliminate All of the Above

d. If you are sure 2 of the 3 are right – pick All of the Above

Longer Answers
a. Often the correct answer is the one with the most information but not always.

Go with your first answer
a. Avoid changing your answer unless you realize you misread the question.

Guessing
a. If there are no penalties for guessing, make an educated guess based on working through the question with steps 1-5.

b. If you aren't sure of the answer, you can narrow it down

   i. Cross off the ones that aren't right.

   ii. If the answer is something you have never seen before, cross it off.

   iii. For number answers, cross off the high and low numbers.

   iv. If two numbers are opposite, one is likely the right answer.

c. If you can't make up your mind between two answers:

   i. Use visualization.

   ii. See the 2 answers as correct.

   iii. Decide which one "feels" right in your gut and go with that one.

Words You Should Avoid

The Law of Belief states that whatever you believe, with feeling, becomes reality.

What we say to ourselves becomes what we believe and words have great power to make us believe either in ourselves or in our own weaknesses.

These are some words you should avoid and some replacements that will give you stronger belief in yourself.

I Can't

I can't do something often means I won't try something because I am afraid to fail. Switch "I can't" with "I can't YET". Adding "yet" lets you know that it is possible.

Problem

Problems are negative. Instead of saying that you have a problem, say you have an opportunity. Most said there was a problem — candlelight was hard on the eyes. Edison knew he had an opportunity and created the light bulb (and buckets of money).

If

We use if as a qualifier to give us room to not achieve our goal. If I make the team... If I make this shot... If I get a good mark on this test... We need to change those IFs to WHEN. Be positive, have confidence. Say WHEN I make the team and make sure your beliefs match your goals.

Just

Don't minimize your accomplishments and successes by using the qualifier "JUST". I "just" got a 78 — and then don't mention that this is the highest mark you have ever got.

Someday I'll

People always say "Someday I'll" (get in shape, talk to that person, do whatever). You won't find Someday on the calendar and so don't get stuck on Someday Isle. Instead, just take ACTION and do it now!

Why Me?

"Why does this always happen to me?" This is a victim mentality that is just an excuse for not making changes so that it doesn't happen. Remember the Law of Expectation. If it ALWAYS happens, you will find a way to make sure you are right. Instead, change your future.

I Will Try

Saying you will "try" is preparing for a future failure. Try to stand up — you either do or do not, there is no try (Thanks Yoda). Instead, drop the try and just say I WILL!

But What IF...

"But what if this happens, I'll fail." This is the voice of fear working at you, nibbling away at your confidence. Be an inverse paranoid — imagine the universe is setting out to do amazing things for you, not to you. Sure look for obstacles and then change it to, "if this happens, I will do this. Be positive and proactive.

Success Log

How successful are we?

Memories are linked to emotion so we remember emotional events more than we remember events that don't provoke memory.

You walk down the hall a thousand times perfectly. Then you trip once and your books go all over the place. You are embarrassed, ashamed, and scared you will be teased. Which one do you remember — 1000 successes or 1 failure?

We are always more successful than we think because we treat the 1000 walks down the hall as "just what we are supposed to do" and the 1 trip as a huge failure.

We need to start treating the "just what we are supposed to do" things as true successes.

What do we consider a success?

We also qualify our successes. We say, "sure, I sunk the basket but it took me 23 tries." It doesn't matter how many times it takes. It took Edison 10,000 tries to get the lightbulb but we still think of him as a huge success.

Don't worry about how long it takes, focus on the fact that you succeeded. You are amazing because you succeeded – even if you are the last one in your class to succeed, you are still a success. Your only competition is you!

When is the only time we fail – when we stop trying and give up. That is a failure.

Why is it important to remember our successes in our Success Log?

We already know that we forget our successes and remember our failures. At the back of the this book, write down all your successes (no matter how small you think they are) so you don't forget them.

When you are facing some new challenge take a few moments to go back over your Success Log. This will give you the opportunity to see how you have achieved many successes in the past. You can build your self-esteem and confidence by going over these successes.

The past successes might even be very similar to the current challenge and hold the solution you are looking for!

> **Remember**
> No success is too small to put on the list.
> Be proud of your successes and write them down every day.

My Success Log – I was successful at:

My Success Log – I was successful at:

My Success Log – I was successful at:

My Success Log – I was successful at:

My Success Log – I was successful at:

My Success Log – I was successful at:

My Success Log – I was successful at:

My Success Log – I was successful at:

_____

_____

_____

_____

_____

_____

_____

_____

_____

_____

_____

_____

_____

_____

_____

Habit Tracker
New Habit _____

Use these sheets to track your new habits. Cross off each day you are successful with the new habit and try not to break the chain. Don't worry if you miss a day, just start the chain over again.

September	October	November	December	January	February	March	April	May	June	July	August
1	1	1	1	1	1	1	1	1	1	1	1
2	2	2	2	2	2	2	2	2	2	2	2
3	3	3	3	3	3	3	3	3	3	3	3
4	4	4	4	4	4	4	4	4	4	4	4
5	5	5	5	5	5	5	5	5	5	5	5
6	6	6	6	6	6	6	6	6	6	6	6
7	7	7	7	7	7	7	7	7	7	7	7
8	8	8	8	8	8	8	8	8	8	8	8
9	9	9	9	9	9	9	9	9	9	9	9
10	10	10	10	10	10	10	10	10	10	10	10
11	11	11	11	11	11	11	11	11	11	11	11
12	12	12	12	12	12	12	12	12	12	12	12
13	13	13	13	13	13	13	13	13	13	13	13
14	14	14	14	14	14	14	14	14	14	14	14
15	15	15	15	15	15	15	15	15	15	15	15
16	16	16	16	16	16	16	16	16	16	16	16
17	17	17	17	17	17	17	17	17	17	17	17
18	18	18	18	18	18	18	18	18	18	18	18
19	19	19	19	19	19	19	19	19	19	19	19
20	20	20	20	20	20	20	20	20	20	20	20
21	21	21	21	21	21	21	21	21	21	21	21
22	22	22	22	22	22	22	22	22	22	22	22
23	23	23	23	23	23	23	23	23	23	23	23
24	24	24	24	24	24	24	24	24	24	24	24
25	25	25	25	25	25	25	25	25	25	25	25
26	26	26	26	26	26	26	26	26	26	26	26
27	27	27	27	27	27	27	27	27	27	27	27
28	28	28	28	28	28	28	28	28	28	28	28
29	29	29	29	29		29	29	29	29	29	29
30	30	30	30	30		30	30	30	30	30	30
	31		31	31		31		31		31	31

Habit Tracker
New Habit _____

Use these sheets to track your new habits. Cross off each day you are successful with the new habit and try not to break the chain. Don't worry if you miss a day, just start the chain over again.

September	October	November	December	January	February	March	April	May	June	July	August
1	1	1	1	1	1	1	1	1	1	1	1
2	2	2	2	2	2	2	2	2	2	2	2
3	3	3	3	3	3	3	3	3	3	3	3
4	4	4	4	4	4	4	4	4	4	4	4
5	5	5	5	5	5	5	5	5	5	5	5
6	6	6	6	6	6	6	6	6	6	6	6
7	7	7	7	7	7	7	7	7	7	7	7
8	8	8	8	8	8	8	8	8	8	8	8
9	9	9	9	9	9	9	9	9	9	9	9
10	10	10	10	10	10	10	10	10	10	10	10
11	11	11	11	11	11	11	11	11	11	11	11
12	12	12	12	12	12	12	12	12	12	12	12
13	13	13	13	13	13	13	13	13	13	13	13
14	14	14	14	14	14	14	14	14	14	14	14
15	15	15	15	15	15	15	15	15	15	15	15
16	16	16	16	16	16	16	16	16	16	16	16
17	17	17	17	17	17	17	17	17	17	17	17
18	18	18	18	18	18	18	18	18	18	18	18
19	19	19	19	19	19	19	19	19	19	19	19
20	20	20	20	20	20	20	20	20	20	20	20
21	21	21	21	21	21	21	21	21	21	21	21
22	22	22	22	22	22	22	22	22	22	22	22
23	23	23	23	23	23	23	23	23	23	23	23
24	24	24	24	24	24	24	24	24	24	24	24
25	25	25	25	25	25	25	25	25	25	25	25
26	26	26	26	26	26	26	26	26	26	26	26
27	27	27	27	27	27	27	27	27	27	27	27
28	28	28	28	28	28	28	28	28	28	28	28
29	29	29	29	29		29	29	29	29	29	29
30	30	30	30	30		30	30	30	30	30	30
	31		31	31		31		31		31	31

Habit Tracker
New Habit _____

Use these sheets to track your new habits. Cross off each day you are successful with the new habit and try not to break the chain. Don't worry if you miss a day, just start the chain over again.

September	October	November	December	January	February	March	April	May	June	July	August
1	1	1	1	1	1	1	1	1	1	1	1
2	2	2	2	2	2	2	2	2	2	2	2
3	3	3	3	3	3	3	3	3	3	3	3
4	4	4	4	4	4	4	4	4	4	4	4
5	5	5	5	5	5	5	5	5	5	5	5
6	6	6	6	6	6	6	6	6	6	6	6
7	7	7	7	7	7	7	7	7	7	7	7
8	8	8	8	8	8	8	8	8	8	8	8
9	9	9	9	9	9	9	9	9	9	9	9
10	10	10	10	10	10	10	10	10	10	10	10
11	11	11	11	11	11	11	11	11	11	11	11
12	12	12	12	12	12	12	12	12	12	12	12
13	13	13	13	13	13	13	13	13	13	13	13
14	14	14	14	14	14	14	14	14	14	14	14
15	15	15	15	15	15	15	15	15	15	15	15
16	16	16	16	16	16	16	16	16	16	16	16
17	17	17	17	17	17	17	17	17	17	17	17
18	18	18	18	18	18	18	18	18	18	18	18
19	19	19	19	19	19	19	19	19	19	19	19
20	20	20	20	20	20	20	20	20	20	20	20
21	21	21	21	21	21	21	21	21	21	21	21
22	22	22	22	22	22	22	22	22	22	22	22
23	23	23	23	23	23	23	23	23	23	23	23
24	24	24	24	24	24	24	24	24	24	24	24
25	25	25	25	25	25	25	25	25	25	25	25
26	26	26	26	26	26	26	26	26	26	26	26
27	27	27	27	27	27	27	27	27	27	27	27
28	28	28	28	28	28	28	28	28	28	28	28
29	29	29	29	29		29	29	29	29	29	29
30	30	30	30	30		30	30	30	30	30	30
	31		31	31		31		31		31	31

Habit Tracker
New Habit _____

Use these sheets to track your new habits. Cross off each day you are successful with the new habit and try not to break the chain. Don't worry if you miss a day, just start the chain over again.

September	October	November	December	January	February	March	April	May	June	July	August
1	1	1	1	1	1	1	1	1	1	1	1
2	2	2	2	2	2	2	2	2	2	2	2
3	3	3	3	3	3	3	3	3	3	3	3
4	4	4	4	4	4	4	4	4	4	4	4
5	5	5	5	5	5	5	5	5	5	5	5
6	6	6	6	6	6	6	6	6	6	6	6
7	7	7	7	7	7	7	7	7	7	7	7
8	8	8	8	8	8	8	8	8	8	8	8
9	9	9	9	9	9	9	9	9	9	9	9
10	10	10	10	10	10	10	10	10	10	10	10
11	11	11	11	11	11	11	11	11	11	11	11
12	12	12	12	12	12	12	12	12	12	12	12
13	13	13	13	13	13	13	13	13	13	13	13
14	14	14	14	14	14	14	14	14	14	14	14
15	15	15	15	15	15	15	15	15	15	15	15
16	16	16	16	16	16	16	16	16	16	16	16
17	17	17	17	17	17	17	17	17	17	17	17
18	18	18	18	18	18	18	18	18	18	18	18
19	19	19	19	19	19	19	19	19	19	19	19
20	20	20	20	20	20	20	20	20	20	20	20
21	21	21	21	21	21	21	21	21	21	21	21
22	22	22	22	22	22	22	22	22	22	22	22
23	23	23	23	23	23	23	23	23	23	23	23
24	24	24	24	24	24	24	24	24	24	24	24
25	25	25	25	25	25	25	25	25	25	25	25
26	26	26	26	26	26	26	26	26	26	26	26
27	27	27	27	27	27	27	27	27	27	27	27
28	28	28	28	28	28	28	28	28	28	28	28
29	29	29	29	29		29	29	29	29	29	29
30	30	30	30	30		30	30	30	30	30	30
	31		31	31		31		31		31	31

Habit Tracker
New Habit _____

Use these sheets to track your new habits. Cross off each day you are successful with the new habit and try not to break the chain. Don't worry if you miss a day, just start the chain over again.

September	October	November	December	January	February	March	April	May	June	July	August
1	1	1	1	1	1	1	1	1	1	1	1
2	2	2	2	2	2	2	2	2	2	2	2
3	3	3	3	3	3	3	3	3	3	3	3
4	4	4	4	4	4	4	4	4	4	4	4
5	5	5	5	5	5	5	5	5	5	5	5
6	6	6	6	6	6	6	6	6	6	6	6
7	7	7	7	7	7	7	7	7	7	7	7
8	8	8	8	8	8	8	8	8	8	8	8
9	9	9	9	9	9	9	9	9	9	9	9
10	10	10	10	10	10	10	10	10	10	10	10
11	11	11	11	11	11	11	11	11	11	11	11
12	12	12	12	12	12	12	12	12	12	12	12
13	13	13	13	13	13	13	13	13	13	13	13
14	14	14	14	14	14	14	14	14	14	14	14
15	15	15	15	15	15	15	15	15	15	15	15
16	16	16	16	16	16	16	16	16	16	16	16
17	17	17	17	17	17	17	17	17	17	17	17
18	18	18	18	18	18	18	18	18	18	18	18
19	19	19	19	19	19	19	19	19	19	19	19
20	20	20	20	20	20	20	20	20	20	20	20
21	21	21	21	21	21	21	21	21	21	21	21
22	22	22	22	22	22	22	22	22	22	22	22
23	23	23	23	23	23	23	23	23	23	23	23
24	24	24	24	24	24	24	24	24	24	24	24
25	25	25	25	25	25	25	25	25	25	25	25
26	26	26	26	26	26	26	26	26	26	26	26
27	27	27	27	27	27	27	27	27	27	27	27
28	28	28	28	28	28	28	28	28	28	28	28
29	29	29	29	29		29	29	29	29	29	29
30	30	30	30	30		30	30	30	30	30	30
	31		31	31		31		31		31	31

Habit Tracker
New Habit _____

Use these sheets to track your new habits. Cross off each day you are successful with the new habit and try not to break the chain. Don't worry if you miss a day, just start the chain over again.

	September	October	November	December	January	February	March	April	May	June	July	August
1	1	1	1	1	1	1	1	1	1	1	1	1
2	2	2	2	2	2	2	2	2	2	2	2	2
3	3	3	3	3	3	3	3	3	3	3	3	3
4	4	4	4	4	4	4	4	4	4	4	4	4
5	5	5	5	5	5	5	5	5	5	5	5	5
6	6	6	6	6	6	6	6	6	6	6	6	6
7	7	7	7	7	7	7	7	7	7	7	7	7
8	8	8	8	8	8	8	8	8	8	8	8	8
9	9	9	9	9	9	9	9	9	9	9	9	9
10	10	10	10	10	10	10	10	10	10	10	10	10
11	11	11	11	11	11	11	11	11	11	11	11	11
12	12	12	12	12	12	12	12	12	12	12	12	12
13	13	13	13	13	13	13	13	13	13	13	13	13
14	14	14	14	14	14	14	14	14	14	14	14	14
15	15	15	15	15	15	15	15	15	15	15	15	15
16	16	16	16	16	16	16	16	16	16	16	16	16
17	17	17	17	17	17	17	17	17	17	17	17	17
18	18	18	18	18	18	18	18	18	18	18	18	18
19	19	19	19	19	19	19	19	19	19	19	19	19
20	20	20	20	20	20	20	20	20	20	20	20	20
21	21	21	21	21	21	21	21	21	21	21	21	21
22	22	22	22	22	22	22	22	22	22	22	22	22
23	23	23	23	23	23	23	23	23	23	23	23	23
24	24	24	24	24	24	24	24	24	24	24	24	24
25	25	25	25	25	25	25	25	25	25	25	25	25
26	26	26	26	26	26	26	26	26	26	26	26	26
27	27	27	27	27	27	27	27	27	27	27	27	27
28	28	28	28	28	28	28	28	28	28	28	28	28
29	29	29	29	29		29	29	29	29	29	29	29
30	30	30	30	30		30	30	30	30	30	30	30
31		31		31		31		31		31	31	31

Habit Tracker
New Habit _____

Use these sheets to track your new habits. Cross off each day you are successful with the new habit and try not to break the chain. Don't worry if you miss a day, just start the chain over again.

September	October	November	December	January	February	March	April	May	June	July	August
1	1	1	1	1	1	1	1	1	1	1	1
2	2	2	2	2	2	2	2	2	2	2	2
3	3	3	3	3	3	3	3	3	3	3	3
4	4	4	4	4	4	4	4	4	4	4	4
5	5	5	5	5	5	5	5	5	5	5	5
6	6	6	6	6	6	6	6	6	6	6	6
7	7	7	7	7	7	7	7	7	7	7	7
8	8	8	8	8	8	8	8	8	8	8	8
9	9	9	9	9	9	9	9	9	9	9	9
10	10	10	10	10	10	10	10	10	10	10	10
11	11	11	11	11	11	11	11	11	11	11	11
12	12	12	12	12	12	12	12	12	12	12	12
13	13	13	13	13	13	13	13	13	13	13	13
14	14	14	14	14	14	14	14	14	14	14	14
15	15	15	15	15	15	15	15	15	15	15	15
16	16	16	16	16	16	16	16	16	16	16	16
17	17	17	17	17	17	17	17	17	17	17	17
18	18	18	18	18	18	18	18	18	18	18	18
19	19	19	19	19	19	19	19	19	19	19	19
20	20	20	20	20	20	20	20	20	20	20	20
21	21	21	21	21	21	21	21	21	21	21	21
22	22	22	22	22	22	22	22	22	22	22	22
23	23	23	23	23	23	23	23	23	23	23	23
24	24	24	24	24	24	24	24	24	24	24	24
25	25	25	25	25	25	25	25	25	25	25	25
26	26	26	26	26	26	26	26	26	26	26	26
27	27	27	27	27	27	27	27	27	27	27	27
28	28	28	28	28	28	28	28	28	28	28	28
29	29	29	29	29		29	29	29	29	29	29
30	30	30	30	30		30	30	30	30	30	30
	31		31	31		31		31		31	31

Habit Tracker
New Habit _____

Use these sheets to track your new habits. Cross off each day you are successful with the new habit and try not to break the chain. Don't worry if you miss a day, just start the chain over again.

September	October	November	December	January	February	March	April	May	June	July	August
1	1	1	1	1	1	1	1	1	1	1	1
2	2	2	2	2	2	2	2	2	2	2	2
3	3	3	3	3	3	3	3	3	3	3	3
4	4	4	4	4	4	4	4	4	4	4	4
5	5	5	5	5	5	5	5	5	5	5	5
6	6	6	6	6	6	6	6	6	6	6	6
7	7	7	7	7	7	7	7	7	7	7	7
8	8	8	8	8	8	8	8	8	8	8	8
9	9	9	9	9	9	9	9	9	9	9	9
10	10	10	10	10	10	10	10	10	10	10	10
11	11	11	11	11	11	11	11	11	11	11	11
12	12	12	12	12	12	12	12	12	12	12	12
13	13	13	13	13	13	13	13	13	13	13	13
14	14	14	14	14	14	14	14	14	14	14	14
15	15	15	15	15	15	15	15	15	15	15	15
16	16	16	16	16	16	16	16	16	16	16	16
17	17	17	17	17	17	17	17	17	17	17	17
18	18	18	18	18	18	18	18	18	18	18	18
19	19	19	19	19	19	19	19	19	19	19	19
20	20	20	20	20	20	20	20	20	20	20	20
21	21	21	21	21	21	21	21	21	21	21	21
22	22	22	22	22	22	22	22	22	22	22	22
23	23	23	23	23	23	23	23	23	23	23	23
24	24	24	24	24	24	24	24	24	24	24	24
25	25	25	25	25	25	25	25	25	25	25	25
26	26	26	26	26	26	26	26	26	26	26	26
27	27	27	27	27	27	27	27	27	27	27	27
28	28	28	28	28	28	28	28	28	28	28	28
29	29	29	29	29		29	29	29	29	29	29
30	30	30	30	30		30	30	30	30	30	30
	31		31	31		31		31		31	31

The "Bad Luck" of Soichrio Honda - Bullet Answers

- Honda wanted to sell his piston to Toyota

- He used all his money to build it and failed

- He finally succeeded but had trouble building his factory – but he found a way

- He had trouble getting materials

- but he used discarded gas cans from American fighter pilots

- His factory was destroyed by earthquakes

- He made a motorized bike to be able to get around

- Wrote thousands of letters to get investors in the new company

- He was finally successful and now sells motorcycles and cars around the world

- Honda used perseverance, creativity, and hard work to succeed

www.ingramcontent.com/pod-product-compliance
Lightning Source LLC
Chambersburg PA
CBHW080638170426
43200CB00015B/2883